Restoring America's Neighborhoods

Restoring America's Neighborhoods

How Local People Make a Difference

MICHAEL R. GREENBERG

RUTGERS UNIVERSITY PRESS
New Brunswick, New Jersey, and London

Library of Congress Cataloging-in-Publication Data

Greenberg, Michael R.
    Restoring America's neighborhoods : how local people make a
difference / by Michael R. Greenberg.
        p.   cm.
    Includes bibliographical references and index.
    ISBN 0-8135-2711-2 (alk. paper). — ISBN 0-8135-2712-0 (pbk. :
alk. paper)
        1. Neighborhood—United States. 2. Inner cities—United States.
3. Community organization—United States. 4. Community development,
Urban—United States. 5. Urban policy—United States. I. Title.
HN57.G695 1999
307.3'362'0973—dc21   99-14063
                                                                 CIP

British Cataloging-in-Publication data for this book is available from the British
Library

Manufactured in the United States of America

To my two favorite "A" girls, Amelia and Alexandra

Contents

Preface

IT MAKES SENSE for you to read this book if you answer yes to at least one of the following questions:

1. Am I distressed by television pictures and newspaper stories of children and elderly people living in fear in crumbling buildings in inner-city neighborhoods?

2. Do I feel that it is unfair for waste-management and other undesirable facilities to be disproportionately located in neighborhoods with poor people who have high rates of death, injury, and illness?

3. Do I believe that it is possible for neighborhood leaders, local governments, and nongovernmental organizations to stabilize and improve neighborhoods with only limited support from the federal and state governments?

If you answered no to all these questions, it makes sense for you to consider why you believe the immiseration of people living in battered neighborhoods has no meaning for you.

In 1993, I began to collect information about people and organizations known for successful efforts in neighborhoods battered by drug-related crime, deteriorated buildings, broken-up sidewalks, and toxic waste incinerators and dumps. My previous work showed that some neighborhoods with multiple problems were improving while others were dying as habitable places. Interviews with over a thousand people pointed to local leadership as the only consistent difference between good and bad outcomes.

The present book chronicles the successful efforts of neighborhood leaders and their organizations. When I started the interviews, I did not know what to call these people. As the interviews proceeded, I realized that common labels, such as leader, activist, organizer, director, trendsetter, pioneer, and so on, were inadequate. The people were figuratively and sometimes literally fighting street-by-street for their neighborhoods. I called them "street fighters" and sometimes "leaders." These people make me proud to be an American. After you read this book, you should feel warmer inside and a little prouder to be an American too. If you don't, it is because I've failed to do justice to the street fighters profiled in this book.

New Brunswick, New Jersey
May 1999

Acknowledgments

I'LL BEGIN BY thanking the people who have been interviewed in dozens of neighborhoods. Without their insights this book would not have been written.

I want to thank Karen Reeds of Rutgers University Press for encouraging me to write a sequel to *Environmentally Devastated Neighborhoods: Perceptions, Policies, and Realities*. Marlie Wasserman, the Director of Rutgers University Press, pushed me to improve my writing. I thank her for her persistence. My colleague Dona Schneider, the coauthor of the first book, my colleague Frank Popper, and my friend Paula Hartz read every chapter of this book. Their comments were invaluable.

George Dawson helped me with the interviews for chapters 2, 3, 5, 8, and 9. I could not have written the book without George's help. My wife, Gwen, helped with the interviews for chapter 4 and for many years has given her moral support for my research about stressed neighborhoods. My daughter Heather Wilkerson and her husband, Jefferson, assisted with the interviews for chapter 7. Yossef Blum, a senior at Yeshiva University in New York City, helped with chapter 6.

I am grateful to George Carey, Leonard Zobler, Douglas McManis, and William Vickrey of Columbia University for challenging me to learn multiple research methods. My parents, Sidney and Mildred Greenberg, raised me in the South Bronx and moved me to Yonkers, where they urged me to use my brain rather than my limited brawn. They, along with my uncle Sol Saletra, shared their unedited feelings about people and neighborhoods with me.

My greatest debt is to the local leaders who invited me into their homes, workplaces, and lives. I dedicate this book to them.

Restoring America's Neighborhoods

| Chapter 1 | # Neighborhood Quality and Street Fighters |

Neighborhood Killers

WE LIKE PASSION in our lives, but not in our neighborhoods. Americans want their neighborhoods quiet, stable, tidy, and, above all, safe. Since eighty-five people out of one hundred rate their neighborhood as of "excellent" or "good" quality, most Americans seem to be getting what they want.[1] The remaining 15 percent rate their neighborhood as of "fair" or "poor" quality. I call them "multiple hazard" or "stressed" neighborhoods because they contain so many dangers. This description of a poor-quality neighborhood from an elderly African American resident of Chester, Pennsylvania, is illustrative:

> I live in the worst neighborhood anyone could live in. Drive-by shootings, car thefts, young children destroying property, not enough lights, unruly patrons from the local bar. There are drugs, trash in the streets, and odors from rotting garbage. Our property value is zero. This neighborhood is a hazard, and none of the residents deserve it.

I have been in his neighborhood three times. It makes me feel like I'm sitting on top of a ticking time bomb; I never relax. Among the more than three thousand Americans I have surveyed across the United States during the last ten years, I have yet to find anyone who rated his or her neighborhood as of good or excellent quality when the combination of unsafe conditions and physical decay are present.

Garbage and hazardous-waste incinerators, chemical factories, sewage plants, airplane flight paths, and other locally unwanted land uses, known by the memorable acronym LULUs, also can kill a neighborhood. Peeking through the drawn blind of her living room at the heavy traffic on Route 1 in Rahway, New Jersey, a woman I call Myra Williams reacted with anger when I discussed the construction of a garbage incinerator in her neighborhood:

> When I first moved into this neighborhood in 1992, it was the end of a nightmare for me. But that [expletive] incinerator has changed everything. I can't even let my eight-year-old play out front anymore. I'm afraid he'll chase a ball into the street and get run over by a garbage truck. Good-quality people are leaving, and the neighborhood will fill up with the drug element.

Myra Williams feels that a manmade piranha has been let loose in her neighborhood and that no one will move in if they have the option of living elsewhere.

The most perilous conditions for neighborhood quality are almost always crime, physical decay, and LULUs. In some neighborhoods, packs of roaming dogs and rats terrorize people. In others, floods, winds, waves, mudslides, and other natural hazards can destroy neighborhoods in a matter of hours. In the most isolated rural areas, people may be so distressed by their distance from emergency medical care that they feel vulnerable, perceiving that their lives are threatened and the quality of their community diminished.

Amenities do not protect a neighborhood against perilous conditions. Putting up a sign near schools that says, "Drugs not permitted near school," adding some new benches in the park, or even building a new park, does not fool residents. They have to be shown that crime is being controlled, that the streets are being kept clean, that housing is being rehabilitated, and that odors, visual blight, and other offending effluvia from LULUs are being addressed. Take the case of a woman who rated her neighborhood as of "good quality" despite living within one-quarter mile of one of the worst hazardous-waste landfills in the United States:

> I came from Camden [New Jersey], where there was crime, dirt, and stripping of cars and houses. Yes, the landfill scared me. But I went to meetings where they showed us that the water we drink is safe, and they've lined the landfill so it won't leak anymore, and they pump out and clean the toxins. The landfill is really not on my mind anymore.

Because perilous conditions kill neighborhoods, I focus every chapter of this book on people who are engaged in the struggle against them. In most of the interviews I conducted, I asked the people to think about what they would concentrate on if crime, physical decay, and LULUs were not an issue. They consistently answered, "Educating children and providing jobs."

What You Should Get from This Book

You should finish this book with insights about the kinds of people and organizations that successfully devote themselves to combating neighborhood killers and about the policies that these leaders use in the struggle. I emphasize the process of interaction between leaders and policies, not the facts about the policy. For example, I want you to understand why religious institutions are playing such important roles in housing and environmental justice, and how buzzwords such as "reinventing government" have an effect on policy development. This deliberate choice to focus on leader and policy interaction rather than on policy facts is due to the short life of policies in the United States. What survives policy changes is the ability of leaders to view every policy shift, good or bad at first glance, as a chance to do good.

Regarding leadership, we lack insights about people because we focus too much attention on their demographic characteristics and not enough on their personality and emotions. Race, income, formal education, gender, and other personal characteristics that are measured by government statistics do not matter much. Personality is what matters.[2] Neighborhood leaders are optimistic and believe that their efforts to improve neighborhood quality will succeed. They reach out for help so often that they have an amazing ability to handle stress. While many of them lack a college education, street fighters are smart about process, that is, how to get things done. They learn fast—especially from mistakes, probably because they cannot afford to make many. Lastly, nearly every leader I interviewed has had a parent or close relative who was a role model for civic engagement. At least partly due to what they learned from their role models, these individuals had a strong moral and relentless loyalty to their communities.

We also lack a clear picture of what kinds of organizations can innovate on behalf of stressed neighborhoods because we look too often in the wrong places. Money and political influence do not guarantee success or even effort. This book shows that allowing innovative staff to engage actively in fighting for neighborhoods offers a much better chance than restricting staff to implementing existing rules and procedures.

Regarding policies, I provide facts about individual efforts, such as anti-arson programs, housing redevelopment, floodplain planning, the spotted owl controversy, environmental-justice movements, brownfields, pollution prevention, and other policy outcomes. But battered neighborhoods need to take advantage of multiple-policy opportunities. Neighborhood leaders recognize that it is not possible to substantially upgrade a stressed multiple-hazard neighborhood unless all the neighborhood killers are addressed. Neighborhood quality is not going to measurably improve as a result of reducing the odor from the smelly petroleum storage tanks if the neighborhood also has drug-related crime and decaying streets and buildings. Nor will a police sweep to rid the neighborhood of drugs help in the long run if garbage is not picked up and industrial odors permeate the neighborhood. The reason for emphasizing this point is that most governmental and nongovernmental organizations have responsibility for only one element. They look at neighborhood problems through narrow lenses and often in sterile, stereotyped ways. Nearly every local leader interviewed in this book clearly sees the relationships among unsafe conditions, physical decay, and LULUs. Many possess a real genius for converting policies conceived to address one problem into opportunities to address all of them. You will read about neighborhoods whose leaders started with an education program that became a housing program. And you will read about a neighborhood where the housing program came first and the education program later.

Letting Loose Neighborhood Killers

The processes that have let loose and sustained neighborhood killers are embedded in every neighborhood in the United States, but they are most visible in our inner cities. I know this from personal experience, as well as from research, because I was raised in one inner-city neighborhood that had been left for dead. My South Bronx neighborhood is a place where our society discards undesirable people and unwanted land uses.

During the 1950s, it was a safe place, with spacious apartments and what seemed to me like a hundred kids playing stickball, softball, football, three-box baseball, and king of the hill, and learning how to do tricks with a yo-yo. We lived about a ten-minute walk from Yankee Stadium, where the Yankees played, and a twenty-minute walk from the Polo Grounds, where the New York Giants (baseball and football) played.

But in the 1950s, the suburbs north of New York City were opened by federally funded roads, and housing was built. Most of the people from the South Bronx, including my family, moved to the suburbs, taking their middle-income buying and political power with them. Poorer people moved into my old South Bronx neighborhood; drug trafficking and gangs proliferated. The former site of the Polo Grounds is now a public-housing project with a high incidence of murder. The baseball Giants moved to San Francisco, the football Giants moved to New Jersey, and the Yankees keep threatening to move out of the South Bronx. My old neighborhood terrifies most middle-class people.

The deterioration of this neighborhood—from excellent to poor and stressed—is being repeated in thousands of poor urban and rural areas across the United States. These neighborhoods have lost people, wealth, jobs, and political clout to the suburbs. By delivering massive numbers of votes in support of Democratic party candidates, big-city neighborhoods have had tremendous political leverage, which they have turned into jobs and social programs.[3] In 1968, President Richard Nixon began to undermine the urban political agenda. His administration reallocated money from national War on Poverty programs, which focused on cities, to state and local governments, which used the funds to operate and maintain their budgets rather than to address neglected city neighborhoods. The national politics of the 1990s are suburban. Middle-class suburban residents now dominate the U.S. population in numbers and wealth. They do not want to pay welfare, bus children to achieve integration, or in other ways continue the so-called "liberal agenda" of the 1950s and 1960s.[4] Neighborhoods like my old South Bronx are viewed by many in power as leeches that are sucking the resources that the United States needs in order to compete in a global economy.

Keeping a Stressed Neighborhood Alive

Controlling conditions that kill neighborhoods is a daunting long-range effort. Five steps are critical as interim objectives that will keep a neighborhood breathing.

One is to *maintain property*. Building codes need to be enforced so that sound buildings don't become dilapidated and dilapidated buildings don't become a peril to the neighborhood. Second, *essential services such as fire, police, and medical need to be maintained*, even if local government can rationally argue that fewer services are needed because the population is declining and businesses have closed. Third, *waste management must be maintained*. Trash must be picked up and neighborhoods must not become dumping grounds for illegal hazardous waste and trash. Fourth, *homeless people and those suffering from substance abuse* must be prevented from destroying the neighborhood's value to investors. Livable quarters and other socially acceptable arrangements must be provided for these marginalized people. Fifth, *LULUs must not be situated in neighborhoods that already have more than their share of neighborhood killers*.

Neighborhood Leaders

In many stressed neighborhoods, only the residents can be counted on to care enough to fight for these five stabilizing objectives and to go beyond them to improve neighborhood quality. Who becomes a neighborhood leader willing to fight thugs, bureaucrats, businesses, and others who have an interest in dumping some LULU in the neighborhood, driving a road through it, or leveling part of it for a new parking garage? Robert Putnam has done the most comprehensive studies of citizen participation.[5] Using national databases, he observed that citizen participation has decreased. While not certain of the cause, he attributes much of it to increased television watching, and less of it to financial and time pressure and loss of neighborhood identity. Regarding demographic characteristics, Putnam observes that older and more educated Americans are the most likely to be engaged. He also observes that civic engagement is associated with trust of governing institutions.

While these observations may be true of Americans as a whole, surveys of inner-city neighborhoods do not support all of Putnam's findings. For example, a study of Harlem (NYC) found that older African American females were the neighborhood leaders.[6] While not well-educated as measured by formal schooling, and not trusting New York City government, these women had assumed leadership in the stressed community. My surveys of residents of public-housing projects and other stressed neighborhoods are consistent with those of Leavitt and Saegert.[7] They found the strongest predictors of activism to be lack of trust in authorities (especially outside authorities), belief in the need to protect future generations against technology, personal optimism, and confidence in their efforts to protect their neighborhoods.[8] Activists were also more likely to be older, have slightly more formal education, and hold stronger religious beliefs. During the 1980s, activism grew rapidly in the United States, especially in less affluent places. People tell me this occurred because they were angry at living in stressed neighborhoods and at feeling that those in authority were not doing much about it.

Local Government and Nongovernmental Organizations

The authority most people expected to rely on was local government. Local government has the ability to help save neighborhoods and the ability to destroy them through indifference, incompetence, and hostile action. Part of the reason that so many neighborhoods are struggling is because local government has not been ready to assume the responsibility dropped on it by the national and state governments. Local governments may also fear that neighborhood leaders could become political rivals in the future.

Daniel Monti concludes that in most cities a situation has to be desperate before government will act.[9] When it does act, it may be to starve stressed neighborhoods so that the neighborhoods can be devalued to the point where they can be leveled and renewed. Alexander Garvin, a member of the New York City Planning Commission and Deputy Commissioner for Housing, observes that, when local government wants to improve neighborhood quality, good planning and adequate funding are necessary but insufficient. The really successful public projects, he demonstrates with examples, allow their staff to act as innovators and entrepreneurs, not paper-trail followers (see chapters 6 and 8).[10]

Nongovernmental organizations (NGOs) have stepped in to fill voids left by government and business, especially in rehabilitating and building housing, fighting for environmental justice in neighborhoods where LULUs are concentrated, and creating jobs. Their most notable contribution has been in housing. In 1983, the last major federally sponsored multifamily housing project ended (see chapters 2, 3, and 8). The Reagan administration slashed HUD's budget and switched most of its funding to tenant-based certificates and voucher subsidies that allowed people to move from public-housing projects to other locations. Some small programs for construction continued for the disabled, the elderly, and rural residents. In addition, block grants were provided to state and local governments for a range of housing and neighborhood development activities. Finally, the Tax Reform Act of 1986 provided incentives for building in poor neighborhoods. But all of these small programs require multiple financing sources as well as cooperation among government, business, and the community. Nonprofits have stepped in to provide loans, equity, grants, financial assistance, and salary subsidies. Their organizational abilities, perhaps, are their most important contribution.[11]

Paul Grogan, president of the Local Initiatives Support Corporation, the largest nonprofit community-development support organization, notes that his organization always works through a local organization. The nonprofit's role, he asserts, is to help the neighborhood organization overcome its political and financial isolation.[12]

But the community has to have contacts. R. Gittell prepared case studies of four small cities that had struggled to rebuild their job base: Lowell (Massachusetts), New Bedford (Massachusetts), Jamestown (New York), and McKeesport (Pennsylvania). He listed ten elements of success. The first was "local leadership able to engage the citizenry and to relate to federal, state, private, and foundation groups."[13]

Federal and State Government

Neighborhoods cannot count on federal and state governments for the kind of financial support and creative ideas that existed decades ago. Besieged by regional, economic, ideological, and other special interests, the federal government struggles over every domestic policy. It no longer has the political heart to lead on domestic issues and maybe cannot do so competently because so many key federal agencies have been enfeebled by budget cuts and political interference during the last two decades.

In his book *Miles to Go,* Senator Daniel Patrick Moynihan of New York states that the era of active government, big business, big labor, and big plans has been replaced by one of decentralization of business and power.[14] Michael Stegman, former assistant secretary for development and research at Housing and Urban Development (HUD), has previewed what we can expect from the federal government. Asserting that the days of "made in Washington" solutions are gone, he argues that HUD's strategy calls for bottom-up planning and collaboration and much less federal funding. The federal role, Stegman states, will be to provide funds and some technical assistance, such as "how to" conferences, to states, local governments, and entrepreneurs.[15]

The analogy I use for the federal government's assistance to stressed neighborhoods is an old piggy bank. There are coins inside, but they are hard to get out. If you can get them out without breaking the bank, you'll find there are fewer coins than you thought, and they are worth less than you hoped. Don't misinterpret me. Many people in the federal government care about stressed multiple-hazard neighborhoods and their residents. But it is hard for them to accomplish much in the 1990s, and what they can accomplish requires working cleverly with their counterparts at the state, local, and community levels (see chapters 4 and 7).

Don't expect much from state governments. The "new federalism" movement, started in the 1980s, in which authority and funds were moved from the federal government to the states, was based on the premise that states were closer than the federal government to local problems and could therefore make decisions that were more appropriate for state residents. The idea makes sense on paper. Yet it has not worked well in reality because most states, especially poor and politically conservative ones, rather than building their own administrative and technical staff in response to an increasing workload, have reduced them. With a few exceptions, states are less able to formulate and implement technically sound policy than they were twenty years ago. The smaller staffs focus on avoiding making mistakes that might be second-guessed. Many of the best and most thoughtful people have left state government as a result of pressure, countless reorganizations, and the feeling that their careers are being wasted.

State agencies with strong leaders supported by the governor and legislature can be innovative and supportive of neighborhoods. Most state agencies, I believe, will be geared up to meet mandates required to obtain federal funding and meet legal requirements set by courts, but not much more. In other words, they will be mostly mediocre, small piggy banks with only a few coins to be used for innovative approaches.

Myron Orfield challenges my argument.[16] Using Minnesota as a case, he argues that a coalition of poor inner cities, inner-ring suburbs experiencing decline, and poor suburbs with underfunded tax bases and lots of schoolchildren can form coalitions to pass legislation for tax sharing. I'm pleased to see that Minnesota can negotiate with its state legislature to find a way to support its inner cities. Such an approach might work in a few other states, such as Massachusetts, New Jersey, New York, and Wisconsin. But I'm highly skeptical about the widespread application of regional solutions. I'd love to be wrong.

In contrast with Orfield's commendable effort to reinvigorate regional government and politics on behalf of stressed neighborhoods, the regional effort I have become all too familiar with during the last two decades is the one which builds a coalition of suburban municipalities to make sure that the landfill, sewage plant, or other LULU gets built in the poor neighborhood. My poster child for regional coalition and government is a poor neighborhood with a maximum security prison, a garbage recycling center, an incinerator, halfway houses, and buildings that used to be hospitals but are now places where people dying from AIDS and other diseases are kept until they die.

Selection of the Case Studies and Organization of the Book

I have collected more than one hundred brief profiles of people and organizations whom I call local leaders or street fighters because their impact is felt in specific neighborhoods. I selected local leaders for this book based on two criteria: they must be diverse in age, race, social class, and geographical location, and half must be local residents (chapters 2–5), the other half individuals who have worked on local problems for federal, state, and local government, as well as nongovernmental organizations (chapters 6–9).

I have briefly described why I chose each local leader to interview and what the interview revealed. I learned about Yvonne Carrington through word-of-mouth and newspaper articles. She was portrayed as someone who had spearheaded a neighborhood revolt against the housing authority and had substantially upgraded the quality of her neighborhood. The redevelopment of the public-housing project that she administers has so changed the complexion of the neighborhood that I imagined that the buildings were laughing at me when I kept staring at them, disbelieving that what I was looking at was "public housing." In chapter 2, I show that Carrington is involved in addressing economic development and education as well as perilous conditions in her neighborhood. Her success amazed me, as did her resolve. She laughed and hugged me when I told her that my grandmother would have called her a "mensch."

I met Reverend Joseph Garlic while walking through the streets of east Elizabeth, New Jersey. The newspapers had reported him as someone who had led housing redevelopment in his poor neighborhood. Describing Garlic as a minister is insufficient, like calling Michael Jordan a basketball player. In chapter 3, I show what true dedication, persistence, and people skills can do for controlling perilous conditions and helping children and job development in a besieged neighborhood. Garlic is a tonic against feelings of powerlessness and helplessness.

Not every perilous condition is found in inner cities. If you have a heart attack or are seriously injured, and if the nearest medical care is hours away, you may die. In chapter 4, I tell the story of David and Jennifer Knowlton, who worked in the northwestern tip of the continental United States as a doctor and lawyer, respectively, for the Native American population. In this remote location, the Knowltons not only made contributions toward establishing a community health system and an employment base, but started a family and learned a great deal about the value of life.

Chapter 5 illustrates what can happen when government decides to locate a facility that the region wants in a neighborhood that does not want it. Ann Parker, Kerri Blanchard, and Robert Carson are three angry residents of a small industrial community. They firmly believe that government picked a bad technology and chose to locate it in the wrong place. Even if you don't believe their claims of deceit, payoffs, and incompetence, even if you dislike their methods for opposing the facility, this chapter underscores the need for honest and open public involvement.

Chapters 6 through 9 focus on government and nongovernment employees whose work for neighborhoods is exemplary. I did not want to do a standard police case study because this country is obsessed with police detectives solving homicides. I wanted to do an arson case study because arson is increasing and has an enormous impact on neighborhood quality, arguably even a greater impact than drug-related homicide. Jon Bozich, William Peck, and James Bush have been fighting arson in Detroit for more than ninety years collectively. The three have had to endure sites of charred bodies and deal with an assortment of criminals who are stupid, greedy, vengeful, and vicious. The excitement and frustrations they feel, and their dedication as architects and implementers of the Detroit Fire Department's efforts to control arson, are described in chapter 6. Detroit's success at controlling some of the most devastating types of arson is testimony to the success of reinventing local government.

Floods, tornadoes, hurricanes, and other natural hazards have become neighborhood killers in the United States. In chapter 7, I tell the story of nine members of the Federal Emergency Management Agency (FEMA) in Kansas City. These nine show that the threat of natural hazards is real, that we need to take it more seriously, and that the federal government cannot do the job without support from state and local governments, nongovernmental organizations, and the public. Most important, they demonstrate that federal employees can successfully engage with their state and local counterparts as well as the public to expedite recovery from disasters and reduce future risks.

If you think local government is a haven for dull and uncaring bureaucrats, you'll be shocked by Alan Mallach. As a city planner, Mallach has been central to the development and implementation of major innovations in housing and land use planning. But what stands out in chapter 8, even more than his intellectual and organizational skills, is his unambiguous sense of right and wrong. For the last decade, Mallach has applied this sense to counter perilous conditions in Trenton, New Jersey.

Chapter 9 starts in New York City and ends in San Diego. It focuses on Charles Lee, who directs the United Church of Christ's Environmental Justice Program, which is national in scope and interacts with many other organizations. Lee, whom I have known for years, has been a major player in the national environmental-justice movement. After explaining what his organization was fighting for, he suggested that we do case studies in North Carolina and San Diego. These studies present the on-the-street realities of environmental justice in two imperiled places.

I wrote an epilogue to provide updates on the people and the neighborhoods that are the centerpieces of this book. Some have continued to fight for their neighborhoods even more vigorously; others have been forced to stop because of personal reasons. Within each of the eight case-study chapters, I describe the people and organizations, provide background information about the community, focus on one or more key efforts made to improve neighborhood quality, discuss accomplishments, and present policy issues that need to be addressed. For the book as a whole, my original intent was to focus each chapter on a specific perilous condition and solution. I started with that premise, but the street fighters didn't let me stick to my plan. They kept on asserting—correctly, of course—that these problems and solutions were intertwined. Every chapter has something to say about perilous conditions and environmental justice. In addition, almost every chapter has something to say about jobs and education.

Life from Death:
Chapter 2   Public Housing in Chester

Figure 1. Yvonne Carrington, manager, Ruth Bennett Homes. *Photo courtesy of the Carrington family.*

O<small>N</small> A<small>UGUST</small> 16, 1988, Carla Juanita Carrington was on her way home from helping the cheerleading coach at Chester High School when she was hit by a stray bullet fired by a local teenager. An honor student about to leave for college, seventeen-year-old Carla died the next day. Her tragic death sparked the transformation of the Ruth Bennett Homes from a rat-infested and horribly neglected complex of almost 400 housing units to a 270–unit apartment community with new peaked roofs, brightly colored entrances, remodeled kitchens, and landscaped lawns. The Ruth Bennett Homes looks like a garden apartment complex for people of modest means—nothing like the standard American image of public housing.

The transformation of the Bennett Homes was directed by Yvonne Carrington, Carla's mother.

> Carrington: My daughter's death was a wake-up call to me. I was trying to understand it, to accept her death. Why would she get killed a few months after her graduation, and on her way to college? I figured out that God wanted me to do what I was best at and in this community. That's the only way I can accept my daughter's death.

The public-housing project was literally rotting beneath the residents.

> Carrington: The people here didn't seem like they were doing anything. When they [the residents] talked about organizing the Ruth Bennett and they put my name up, I started to walk out the door. They said: "Just try it out for a couple of months, and if you don't want to do it, we'll let the vice-president take over." I'm sure I was motivated by the spirit of my baby. She was the real activist. She would tell me all these details about the bad conditions in the community; she used to get so upset. She always wanted to come back [after college] and do some-thing for the kids and older people right here.
>
> Now, she wasn't perfect. She was a seventeen-year-old child. But my God, I didn't expect her to be snatched away from life like that. One time I even blamed my other daughter for this because she [Yvonne's older daughter] was with her when Carla was shot. I ask the Lord to forgive me for that every day. I kept it inside so long that I developed a nervous-related intestinal disease. If I didn't do what I did in this community, I might have been out there on crack or something.

Deep Roots in Chester

Yvonne Carrington's description of her role models sounds like a his-tory of Chester.

> Carrington: All of my family is from Chester, with the excep-tion of my great-grandmother. My great-grandfather used to

walk from here to work in the steel mill. I remember this place when it was an open field. I remember when they tore down my family home to build this place in the early 1950s.

We were a close-knit family. We were raised to share everything. My family always worked and got involved to keep the community thriving. I always was committed to the place. My great-grandmother, Evangeline Boyd, she was always involved in doing things for the kids of the community, and I would say that's where I come closest to getting a lot of in-stincts for helping.

Throughout the interview, Yvonne showed little sympathy for people who are lazy and who blame everybody else for their problems. She attributes her attitude to working with the blind.

Carrington: I was really inspired by the blind people I worked for. I used to say, "How could anybody in the United States be a lazy bum after you go there and see these blind people?" These people could not see, and they went to work every day. They never made money like us. The money they made was a joke. They were realistic. They did what they could with what they had. They didn't whine or complain.

Roderick Powell is a life-skill education instructor at the Delco Blind Sight Center in Chester.

Powell: I met her in 1978. Mrs. Carrington is a beautiful person. I think that her experience working with the blind taught her sensitivity. She taught me how to advocate. I learned so much from her. She taught me how to stand up for myself and to stand up for other people. She's a community leader. She's totally made a difference in Chester.

From Fighting the Housing Authority to the Brink of Ownership

At the time of her daughter's death, Yvonne and her neighbors had good reason to be angry about their living environment.

Carrington: The first big meeting was at the Ruth Bennett. We met with HUD representatives. We took pictures of one house.

> It was horrible. She [the tenant] had many [ten to twelve] people living in a two-bedroom apartment. The place was immaculate, it was so neat, it was as neat as a pin. But she had a big hole in the wall, and the next apartment was vacant. We looked in the crawl spaces, and there were rats, human feces, raw sewage all over the place, inside and outside. In other apartments the toilets didn't flush, and we had roaches all over the place. There are some bad apples [people] here, but it is not like you see on television. These people were trying to keep their apartments neat, but the money for maintenance was going everywhere except where it was supposed to go. We weren't going to take it anymore, so we took it to court [in 1990]. They [the local court] threw it out.

Angry, Yvonne and her neighbors sought help. Said Carrington, "We got ourselves educated about this problem. Carolyn Saunders was the one who really helped us." Saunders, a community organizer with the local legal aid services, advised the residents to ask Judge Norma Shapiro of the U.S. District Court for Eastern Pennsylvania to hear the case.

> Carrington: She [Judge Shapiro] really aided us. When she first came here, she said she couldn't see how HUD could deny the filth here.

Although the Chester Housing Authority was the immediate target of the suit, Yvonne blamed HUD.

> Carrington: The Chester Housing Authority did what HUD told them to do. HUD, to me, was the real culprit. HUD kept sending us people that were incompetent—they wouldn't fix anything. You could not believe all the hearings we went to, and what we put on the record. Some of the things were disgusting, and we hated assembling the information. But we were sick and tired of seeing roaches. And I just said, "I've had it." When you flushed the toilet, roaches would float to the top.

Judge Shapiro ruled in favor of the tenants in 1993.

> Carrington: Judge Shapiro declared this place "troubled, unsafe, unsanitary, and unfit to live in." She said she couldn't figure out how these consultants could have taken the money and done so

little. She said, "They should have torn them [the projects] all
down."

But Yvonne and her neighbors did not want the projects demolished—something they felt HUD wanted. They wanted to stay in their
homes. So they asserted that properly trained residents could maintain
the projects.

> Carrington: We argued that the maintenance people never had
> the proper training. You could never run a place like this with
> 390 units, without proper maintenance.

Judge Shapiro accepted the tenants' argument. She turned management of the complex over to the residents. Judge Shapiro appointed
former New York City housing official Robert Rosenberg as receiver for
the project, to supervise its rehabilitation. The *New York Times* reported
that when Rosenberg first visited the site, he found widespread deterioration, an unresponsive maintenance system, grounds littered with
glass and garbage, crumbling interiors, and such bad bookkeeping that
rents unpaid for two years were being forgiven.[1]

> Carrington: One of the first things we did was to apply for
> proper funding. We got a planning grant [which would lead to
> tenant ownership]. Mr. Anthony Lewis, president of the
> Housing Association of Delaware Valley, helped us with a
> feasibility study, worker training. He helped us with a survey to
> find out what the residents wanted.
>
> The HOPE I planning grant [from HUD—see below for a
> discussion] was critical for us. We had to get all our ducks in a
> row. We had to be trained. We went to Atlanta [Georgia] to
> find out what was expected. We had training for economic
> development, social services, and so on. I learned a lot and
> made many contacts. My title is social services coordinator, but
> I do economic development as well. We had training for
> prevention of drug abuse and intervention.
>
> Michael, you've got to tell people that this is comprehen-
> sive redevelopment, not just housing. When we finally got all
> of this preliminary training and planning done, we picked a
> modernization committee, we picked an architect. Everything

you see here, the tenants picked 85 percent of it. This was
called a "total-gut-rehab."

The Ruth Bennett Homes reconstruction was completed by the end
of 1997 at a total cost of $20 million. While emphasizing the positive,
Carrington did not try to pretend that getting the tenants to work together was easy.

> Carrington: We had a big meeting yesterday. We still have
> some problems to shake off. We had feuding every now and
> then about whether to emphasize the lawsuit or opt for the
> funding. But we always managed to get back together. It really
> has paid off. We're going to redo every last one of the houses. A
> couple of years ago, we didn't think we were going to see this
> until the year 2000.

Nor is she happy about the way all the money was spent. She was
particularly upset with the consultants.

> Carrington: Before they even broke ground in the Bennett,
> they had spent $6 to $7 million on consultants. I'd love to get
> those scoundrels. Think about all the things we could have
> built, all the economic development we could have been
> involved in with another $6 to $7 million.

Despite the inside arguments that she told us kept her up many
nights and the consultants whom she despises, George Dawson and I
could see from Yvonne's short tour of the complex striking evidence of
change in the physical plant. Instead of everyone being shoved into a
single design, residents were permitted to pick from a series of alternative designs. The net result is that the Ruth Bennett complex has 275
units rather than the 390 it began with.

Yvonne fully expects the tenants to own the housing project within
one year.

> Carrington: We want to get home ownership. HUD has trained
> us to eventually take over. It is a beautiful plan. The home-
> ownership piece is the best part HUD put in. HUD wants to get
> rid of this responsibility. They don't want to be bothered with
> public housing anymore. You would not believe the fighting
> and talks and sleep that we all lost over this, but in a year we

can have a choice of who wants to own homes. It is only just that the first one of these should be named after Ruth Bennett, who was a nurse, social worker, and concentrated on helping the homeless. Decision-day is coming. D-Day. And anyone who does not want to own a unit or is undesirable, like the drug addict who lives in the complex, is going to be out of here! Once the transfer occurs the complex will operate like a co-op. One strike and you are out. Everybody here wants this place to look like it does out in the suburbs, with flowers, clean yards, and immaculate insides. The key is two words: tenant participation.

We turned to Mayor Aaron Wilson Jr. for a perspective about Yvonne Carrington. The ex-marine was brief and to the point.

Wilson: Yvonne is a good person, she gets along so well with the tenants. She takes so much responsibility, she picked things up as they came along. She's just a giant.

The mayor's comments about public housing in Chester, where the same physical redevelopment process is underway at three other projects, were equally to the point.

Wilson: We have the largest number of people housed in public housing of any city. Public housing is in a holding pattern. It is a necessity because some people have to have a place to live. But we have to get out of the rut that we're in, that is, that public housing is really a dumping ground for the poor. It should be the opposite. If you really qualify, there should be some "perks": the lawns should be manicured, the places immaculate, and so on. We really need to humanize public housing. We need to make residents feel that they are a part of society, rather than make them feel that they are different. These residents must matriculate in the rest of the world. Poverty doesn't equate to stupidity.

Education, Jobs, and Other Issues at the Ruth Bennett Homes

The remaking of the Ruth Bennett Homes is most evident in the buildings, but Yvonne Carrington emphasized the need for extending the new cooperative attitude to education and employment. Said Carrington, "It is all about tenant participation, educating the tenants so they make good decisions instead of relying on government." The group has started a tenant patrol, a program for grandparents focused on physical fitness and nutrition, and a program of friendship with one's neighbors. A friend of Yvonne's started Friends of Carrington in honor of Carla Carrington.

> Carrington: We saw people eating out of trash cans. We couldn't believe it. Ten days before Thanksgiving, we got companies and people to donate food and distributed it. When we had Hurricane Hugo, we went to South Carolina and fed over two thousand people. We were on the front page of USA Today. We just do so many things together. I love these activities.

Protecting children from peril and improving their education are Yvonne's highest priorities.

> Carrington: The [Chester] education department is in receivership. They wanted to close all the schools here and bus the children to the suburbs. They must be out of their minds. What they propose is a disgrace. We have good teachers here. They need to give the teachers the books and programs they had when my family was going to school. They need to do a survey of the students to find out about the special circumstances of the children. They need to give them a small share of the money they are putting into the new prison for hard-core criminals in our city. No education and more criminals? Does that make sense?

Yvonne and her neighbors have started some education projects.

> Carrington: We work with twenty-five to thirty kids. They're called the Ruth Bennett High Steppers, a drill team. My daughter always wanted to do something like this. We have performed as far away as Disneyland in Tomorrow Land and as close as Marcus Hook [the adjacent industrial community just south of Chester].
> When we were at Marcus Hook, everyone was white. They were waiting for the Bennett High-Steppers to come back. When they were walking down the street, I had tears in my eyes. The people were clapping for the kids from the Bennett.

The Ruth Bennett Homes has also set up a tutoring program and has plans to build a Head Start center. The community also cooperates with the Chester School District in a program called Calling Card for Success. Children from the housing projects are taken to places that they have never been before.

Of all the subjects we discussed, Yvonne Carrington is most anxious and frustrated by the status of education in her community because she sees it as the best way for her neighbors to improve the quality of their lives. She absolutely rejects the idea that public-housing projects produce high school drop-outs. Her family tree says it all. Her oldest daughter has an associate degree and serves as office coordinator, or, as Yvonne put its, is "my right-hand man." Her son was in the air force and has a degree from Kansas State University. Her sister has a college degree and teaches, as do her sisters-in-law. Her brother-in-law has a Ph.D. in English and is a retired high school principal. Her niece graduated from college with honors in French and interior design. Yvonne's younger brother has a degree in architectural design, and her middle brother works for Boeing.

Yvonne Carrington, fifty-six years old, did not finish college. She was in college when her daughter was killed.

Carrington: It [college education] is between the Lord and me.

After listening to her articulate her views, I can tell you unequivocally that Yvonne Carrington does not need a college diploma to prove that she is educated.

Regarding the economy and environmental-justice issues, her anger is not well contained.

Carrington: When I was a little girl, you had a shopping area, which included a Sears Roebuck and another big department store. People came from all over to shop here. But the place got into the hands of the wrong people, and most of the right people left. I hate people stereotyping Chester as drugs and incinerators and other garbage because we've got some very productive things going on here. We have two businesses that I manage. I had read an article about how it would be best to get your own people to remove asbestos and lead because they would do it right, since they had to move back here. We took a survey and found out that a lot of young men and women wanted to get into training classes for asbestos and lead cleanup. So I presented this proposal to the Housing Authority. They said I needed a joint business partner. The story is that we were supposed to get black people for a partner. But they were not prepared to fill out all the forms and stuff, so we almost lost the money. So I met with the Housing Authority, and they recommended Joseph Caruso, owner of C&C Construction of Voorhees [New Jersey]. He really went out on a limb for us. I met with him. He donated money to our food programs, paid for certifications. He always paid on time, even though the Housing Authority never paid *him* on time.

Caruso employed fifteen to eighteen people and paid them $13.63 an hour to remove asbestos and lead.

Carrington: Some of the people, they had never seen such money in their life. They worked six to eight months on our development, and now they have similar work in the area.

Joseph Caruso stated his opinion of the joint venture to the *Philadelphia Inquirer:* "I hope that other housing authorities that do renovations made that kind of agreement possible. It's a great symbiotic relationship between the public and private sectors."[2]

The second business is "Make-Build," which has employed about 200 people during the last three years at making repairs, gardening, and janitorial work. Yvonne is looking for other ideas.

Carrington: We're going to give anybody who wants to start a business a microloan. They're going to have to pay it back. We're going to make the decisions on who gets the loans, and I can tell you that it's not going to be any Johnny-come-lately fly-by-night.

Marginalizing Chester

What Yvonne Carrington and her neighbors have accomplished—that is, successfully fighting the federal government in court—would be remarkable in any environment. That this victory was won in Chester is incredible. Chester is among the places in the United States that first felt the full force of the social changes that have occurred in the United

States during the last two decades. It is one of the most economically stressed cities in the country. Once a heavy industrial city of sixty-five thousand, it lost twenty thousand people and more than forty thousand jobs after the Second World War.

The 4.8–square-mile city is located in Delaware County, Pennsylvania. In 1989, the median family income of Chester's families was less than $25,000, or 56 percent of the county's. The U.S. Census Bureau reports data for 151 cities in the northeast United States (comprising Connecticut, Maine, Massachusetts, New Hampshire, New Jersey, New York, Pennsylvania, Rhode Island, and Vermont). Only five cities had a lower median family income than Chester, and only six of the 151 had a higher proportion of income from public assistance.

Chester's population is two-thirds African American, compared to 7 percent for the remainder of Delaware County. On a scale from 0 to 100, where 100 is total segregation, Chester's African Americans typically score about 70; Hispanics score about 45. In addition, Chester's African Americans are poorer, have less access to bank credit, and inherit smaller amounts than do their white counterparts, so their opportunity to locate in nonsegregated areas is limited.

Chester's economy has been so undermined that the city at one time considered cutting street lighting to save money. Instead, however, it accepted a variety of waste facilities and may become the capital of environmental injustice in the United States. Chester has the county garbage incinerator, the plant that treats nearly all of the county's sewage, a facility that treats medical waste, and multiple hazardous-waste incinerators. My colleagues and I surveyed residents of the neighborhoods near these facilities in 1993.[3] More than 40 percent of respondents were greatly disturbed by ten different problems: buildings in dangerous condition; chemical plants; crime; the county trash incinerator; dogs, rats, and other uncontrolled animals; junkyards; litter or trash in the street; motor vehicle noise and heavy traffic; odors or smoke; and petroleum refining and tank farms. In my almost thirty years of working in industrialized neighborhoods, I have never seen as many different kinds of waste-management facilities crammed into a densely packed residential area as I saw in Chester.

In 1996, Chester's citizens sued the Pennsylvania Department of Environmental Protection when the state government issued a permit for another waste facility in Chester. The suit argues that Pennsylvania violated Title VI of the Civil Rights Act, which forbids discriminatory behavior by any agency receiving federal funds. In December 1997, the attorney representing the plaintiffs was informed that they had been given standing to move forward with the case—in other words, they had been granted legal standing to sue. This landmark environmental-justice lawsuit underscores the difficulties Yvonne Carrington and her neighbors face in their efforts to control their beleaguered city: Based on the concentration of waste management facilities, it would be difficult to dismiss the charge. However, the applicants have argued that they did not deliberately choose the area because it was occupied by poor people; they chose it because it was a good site for their businesses. Process equity considerations might support their case.

The environmental-injustice case will not directly impact the work of Yvonne Carrington and her neighbors in the short run. Their neighborhood is located on the western edge of Chester; most of the industrial facilities are located on the eastern edge, more than a mile away. But Yvonne hopes that her approach to controlling perilous conditions will spread to the other housing projects, some of which are much closer to the industrial sites. Furthermore, Chester needs to get out from under the reputation that it is a place to put LULUs that can't easily be put someplace else.

Mayor Wilson had strong feelings about the Chester economy.

> Wilson: We're what they call a "distressed" city. That's when the state steps in because you're so far down in debt. They're working well with us. We had a $10 million deficit when we took office twenty months ago. Since we have only a $20–25 million budget, you can see how bad it was. But we're in good shape now. We have $73 million in new construction underway.

The mayor's optimism is based on Chester's locational advantages. While recognizing that its location on a major river, with modern highways, railroads, and near Philadelphia have brought it LULUs, he has focused instead on what the local government could and was doing to benefit neighborhoods and the residents. A new transportation center is being built with a new stop for Amtrak (the main line connecting

Washington and New York City), jobs are being created along the waterfront, and a state prison is under construction. He expects these to produce more than 25,000 new jobs.

Mayor Wilson laid out a vision in which Chester would be able to create desirable land uses as a result of its history.

> Wilson: Chester was the capital of Pennsylvania. William Penn landed in Chester. We can almost create a Williamsburg here. We have the oldest functioning courthouse in the country.

In addition, the mayor noted that an office building is being built adjacent to Widener University in Chester, and that Drexel University is building a facility in the same area. The mayor is encouraging local utilities to clean up their waterfront areas with brownfields funds so that marinas, restaurants, condos, and other private, market-driven activities will be attracted. He noted that "developers are knocking down our doors to come in." Part of the mayor's ambitious plan is to link the jobs and Chester's low-income residents via bus service. For example: "We have a loop around the Philadelphia airport with United Parcel Service to take workers out there. We're giving the low-income person the first crack at jobs."

Like Yvonne Carrington, Mayor Wilson has little tolerance for people who can work but do not, and he believes that jobs and education are required. He is not a big supporter of welfare, but he feels that the federal government can help in a variety of ways.

> Wilson: We need to create incentives to help create a work ethic. Education and employment are the answers to many of our problems. Right now, crime does pay. It pays very well. Just ask your neighborhood pusher. We have a "weed and seed" program in high-crime areas. A combination of federal, state, and local law enforcement people focus on an area for two years to weed out the criminal element. We have a zero tolerance for crime at the housing projects. The seed part is to get the involvement of the community in policing. But then we need to educate people and create jobs.
>
> Our [national] priorities are messed up. They'll spend $1 million on a baseball player, $3 million on a guy carrying a football, and $5 million on someone shooting a basketball. But the teacher gets paid $25,000 to $30,000, and they raise hell at

us about requests for books and computers. We subsidize Lockheed, Chrysler, cotton, and farming. The moment you ask for money for the poor, everyone screams. The little guy doesn't have a shot. It seems strange that the entire Congress would let it happen. Right now a few really control who wins and loses in this society. People do not understand, especially people in this community, that this is really not a game between Democrats and Republicans. It is a game between winners and losers.

U.S. Government Housing Policy: An Evolutionary Process

Changes in federal housing and welfare policy are both critical to events at the Ruth Bennett Homes. No one I have spoken with disputes Yvonne Carrington's assertion that the U.S. government wants to get out of public housing. In 1930, when the first federal government policy was created, it was intended to help people who temporarily needed housing. Gradually, public housing expanded from way stations to permanent housing for low-income families. In 1955, HUD had a total of 344,000 public-housing units. By 1970, the number was 830,000 and growing. The peak exceeded 1.4 million by 1990. This increase reflects the growing squeeze since the 1980s on homeowners and renters, especially the poor.

Census data show that the overall poverty rate was 11.6 percent in 1980, 12.8 percent in 1989, and 14.2 percent in 1991. In 1992, 14.5 percent of Americans lived in poverty, including 22 percent of all U.S. children. National studies have found that poverty has become more spatially clustered in places like Chester, Detroit, Elizabeth, and Trenton.[4] Studies also show that more than half of all poor renters spend at least half of their resources on rent and utilities, and that many double and triple up in housing.

While the demand for low-income housing increased during the 1980s, the U.S. government decided that building new public housing was not what was needed. New units were expensive, and evidence pointed to high-rise public housing as fostering crime and disease. In 1982, President Reagan's Commission on Housing concluded that the goal of federal housing programs should be to help people, not build housing projects. The government began to substitute a variety of voucher programs for building new projects. The other option was rehabilitation. In 1970, about 85 percent of HUD's assisted units were public housing. By 1990, the proportion had decreased to less than 30 percent.

In essence, Congress and the executive branch have chosen to return the provision of housing back to its capitalist grass roots. From 1980 to 1990, budgets for subsidized housing fell from $25 to $10 billion, and annual subsidized housing starts fell from an average of 175,000 to 20,000. Those funds available for construction were switched from new construction to rehabilitation (over 80 percent in the 1990s compared to only 5 percent during the 1960s).

Analysts calculate that about one-half the support for low-income housing comes from welfare through Aid for Dependent Children. In 1996, the U.S. government dramatically changed its welfare system, reducing the subsidy and the length of time someone could use it, and turned management over to the states. The implications of this policy change on housing are unclear, but a recent survey of all health officers in New Jersey, conducted by the author and colleagues, found a nexus between changes in federal housing, welfare, and health-care management policies in the United States. Overwhelmingly, the health officers' major concern was for the low-income residents of their jurisdictions.[5]

When it was filed, the lawsuit brought by Yvonne Carrington and her neighbors was considered by HUD to be a radical adversarial step. However, HUD's response has softened. The *New York Times* quoted Maryann Russ, then HUD deputy assistant secretary for Public and Housing Operations: "I don't know if this gets things done any faster. But in certain situations, because of a combination of political intransigence and deep-seated suspicions housing residents have about local administrations, this is the only way to bring in a new broom."[6]

Part of this response is doubtless due to the fact that the Republican majority in Congress attempted to dissolve HUD. Failing this, Congress set out to privatize public housing. These changes in housing policy at the national scale coincided with what was happening at the Ruth Bennett. For example, project HOPE (Homeownership of Single Family Homes Program) was instituted. Early evaluations showed that there were fewer people in the HOPE program than had been anticipated, but also that very few of the buyers defaulted on their mortgages or sold their homes. Yvonne Carrington's group was one of the first to receive a HOPE grant.

Tax credits for investing in low-income housing were another potential benefit for a city like Chester. The National Affordable Housing Act of 1990 (NAHA) provided federal matching grants for housing rehabilitation and other purposes. NAHA also created a Family Sufficiency Program (FSP), the goal of which was to coordinate day care, education, job training, and other social services provided to public-housing tenants. This program had the authority to remove gang and drug-related activities from the premises. In 1996, a House-Senate committee negotiated language that would hold local housing authorities to performance standards which, if not met, would lead to private management. In fact, Yvonne Carrington's program for the Ruth Bennett strongly resembles so-called "community service hubs" proposed in the literature as neighborhood facilities that would provide emergency shelter, child care, food, and health-care services.

Overall, over the last two decades three important trends have emerged in U.S. public-housing policy that directly bear on cities like Chester and neighborhoods like Yvonne Carrington's. The U.S. government clearly is pulling back from its previous financial commitment, which was already far less than Europe's. Second, state and local governments and private enterprise involvement has substantially increased. Third, people increasingly understand that adequate housing without adequate education, employment opportunities, and other services is not salutary.

The policy most antithetical to what Yvonne Carrington has been doing is the one that demolishes public-housing projects and scatters their residents. In other words, break up poor neighborhoods, don't invest in them. One argument for the scatter policy is that it helps people leave poverty, escape racism, obtain better schooling, and locate job opportunities not available in the low-income area. Studies have reported that continued contacts between those who leave poor neighborhoods and those who stay "pull down" those who might otherwise escape poverty. Chicago plans to demolish its public-housing projects, construct large, mixed-income residential developments, guarantee the relocation of public-housing project tenants, provide adequate housing for those who want to stay in the neighborhood, and rid neighborhoods of gangs, drugs, and crime.[7]

Mayor Wilson has strong feelings about the need to reform public housing and move people to other locations.

> Wilson: I don't believe in moving people around. It raises problems in other neighborhoods. Some residents believe that Section 8 [relocated] people have horns. But I know if you spend thirty-eight years in a public-housing project, you're talking about four generations. I don't think we can afford to pay for that anymore. The Congress is cutting the budgets. We really need to make people who live in public-housing work and pay some of the money they earn toward the housing. We need to upgrade the quality of public housing. We need to consider options that are wholly or partly market driven. The status quo is not going to be maintained.

Coming Full Circle: From a Personal Tragedy to a Personal Challenge

Is the model worked out by Yvonne Carrington and her neighbors viable? That is, can we transfer the units to the residents and help them set up businesses in the community? Or should the U.S. government let the buildings rot until they are ready to be demolished, while offering the residents the opportunity to relocate to better neighborhoods? Not surprisingly, Yvonne had a strong response to my question about whether her neighborhood should be abandoned and the people scattered to avoid the pull-down effect.

> Carrington: No! People focus too much on the bums. We have a few bad apples here, but we're going to weed them out. I am not going to let anyone take away the dreams of everybody else and my dear daughter. Focus on the high-steppers instead of the bums. You go in their houses—clean, neat, they take care of themselves. They take pride. These kids come from families that were involved with drugs. But they've changed. It's time to be optimistic about these people.

There was more than just a trace of bitter irony and anger in Yvonne Carrington's voice as she continued her response. For her, a pragmatist and realist, the idea of killing her neighborhood smacks of the same kind of stupidity that killed her daughter.

> Carrington: It was a grudge that one of them had two years earlier. The argument was stupid. But my daughter caught that bullet, the night before she was packing to go to college. I had bought all her suitcases and we were ready to do some extra shopping. I was angry because they took my baby away from me. This is why I was asking God, "Why me? Why me?" And then I said to myself, "Why not me?" Everything happens for a reason. Don't let stupid political ideology prevent good people from making something out of their lives. Don't scatter people. Give them a chance to live here. Pull-down may happen in some places, but here it has been pull-up.

Chapter 3

Joseph Garlic: Planting Seeds of Hope in Elizabethport

Figure 2. Reverend Joseph Garlic inside the education center named in his honor, Elizabethport, New Jersey. *Photo courtesy of Reverend Garlic*

REVEREND JOSEPH GARLIC'S ministry is on First Street and Magnolia Avenue, across from a public-housing project in Elizabethport, New Jersey. The ministry does not look like a church, which it is not; nor does it look like a school, a day care center, or a meeting place, which it is. Painted tan, the building, which sort of looks like a store, is so unremarkable that George Dawson and I could not find the door. Fortunately, a ten-to-twelve-year-old, laughing at our obvious bumbling around, showed us the entrance on Magnolia. After thanking him, I stepped inside, eagerly awaiting my second conversation with Joseph Garlic.

My first conversation with Reverend Garlic had been in 1993, when my colleague Dona Schneider and I were walking through the neighborhood. On that day, people on the streets of Elizabethport seemed to be in a hurry. Or maybe they were not interested in talking to two obvious strangers. We got that "don't bother me" look that people give you when they think you're going to annoy them. When we saw a sixty-plus-year-old African American man conversing with a group of children in front of what appeared to be a storefront, we walked over and introduced ourselves. Before long, Reverend Garlic was taking us across the street to show us housing that the ministry had rehabilitated and to describe his ideas about improving the quality of life in Elizabethport.

Beginning of the Elizabethport Presbyterian Mission

More than three years later, in December 1996, George and I stepped inside the door with the goal of learning more about the mission of the Presbyterian Ministry in Elizabeth and especially of its leader, Joseph Garlic. Inside, the dull image of the exterior was quickly forgotten, replaced by bright lights and the giggles of children at play in a large room full of toys. A few feet away, a youth was talking to a man about lowest common denominators. Rod Spearman, Minister Garlic's colleague for the last sixteen years and program director of the center, greeted us. The reverend will be a few minutes late, he says. Spearman asks about the purpose of our visit. When we tell him, he smiles the smile of someone who knows that we're about to hear a good story.

Reverend Garlic arrived about a minute later, and within fifteen minutes I knew that Joseph Garlic was not about to allow George and me to leave with the impression that Garlic was solely responsible for the success of the Presbyterian mission in Elizabethport. Indeed, in order to learn more about Reverend Garlic's role in the center, we later formally interviewed Rod Spearman, as well as Manny Grova Jr., Elizabeth First Ward Council Member; Sister Jacinta Fernandes, director of St. Joseph's Social Service Center in Elizabeth; J. Christian Bollwage, mayor of the City of Elizabeth; Patricia Perkins-Auguste, At-Large City Council Member, Elizabeth; and Hazel Garlic, the reverend's wife.

Joseph Garlic's description of the beginning of Elizabethport Center set the pattern for the interview.

> Garlic: Minister James Goldin Miller, a community-minded white man who was the minister of the largely white Greystone Church came up with the idea for the ministry.

Recognizing that the neighborhood was changing from predominantly white to predominantly African American and Hispanic, Reverend Miller understood that some parishioners were uncomfortable with the young neighborhood children who came to the ministry to play. Rather than abandon the area, Miller persuaded the Presbyterian ministry to build a mission in Elizabethport. Currently, about fifty churches in Union, Middlesex, and Warren counties are involved in supporting the Elizabethport Center.

> Garlic: The presbytery are the people who are responsible for it. They created it. At first they provided 100 percent support. I believe that what has inspired me over the years is that a lot of people in the Presbyterian Church gave a lot of money to see this work. And they gave a lot of time, through volunteers, and a lot of concern. I had the responsibility to make sure that something good happened with the money we were given and something positive happened as a result of the trust they placed in me and the center. That's been my responsibility since 1967.

Though consistently focusing on the efforts of the collective rather than on himself, the reverend did manage to tell us a bit about his personal history. He was born and raised in Woodstown, New Jersey, a town of about three thousand people in rural Salem County, New Jersey. His father was a truck farmer who raised vegetables and had some pigs.

> Garlic: I was a good student, and my mother encouraged me to read as much as possible. My parents were very active in the Baptist church. I loved writing book reports. I guess I wanted to be a lawyer.

Some tidbits of personal history helped us understand how he ended up as a minister in Elizabethport.

> Garlic: When I was young, very young, I had an inclination to go into law, until Mrs. Thompson said to me one day, "Why do you want to go into law? Lawyers lie!" That quashed my ambition. It is something how people can say things to you at

that age, how you remember that, and how that affects your whole life. That's the reason I'm not a lawyer today, because of that comment she made to me. As I said, we were a very religious family. I said, "I don't want to grow up to be a liar." So I didn't go into law.

The local librarian told me that I read the most of all the children, and then she told me that I would make a good janitor when I grew up.

Feeling shut out of white-collar occupations because of the color of his skin, young Joseph moved to Newark to escape the blatant racism. There he became a cabinetmaker and in his words "got a call to the ministry." He never wanted to be a minister with his own parish.

Garlic: I preached in a church in North Carolina, but I have never been a regular minister of my own church. Besides, I was married and had a child. I needed a job. For me, coming to work at this place was a unique opportunity. The people were very supportive. They wanted to see things done. I was my own boss. There are so few of these kinds of ministries in the United States.

Elizabethport

Reverend Joseph Garlic's ministry and home are in Elizabethport, the northeasternmost neighborhood of Elizabeth, New Jersey. The one-half-square-mile neighborhood has about eight thousand people. Nearly all are African and Hispanic American. Many are poor. According to census data, the per capita income of the two census areas that form Elizabethport was less than 40 percent of New Jersey's 1989 average of $18,714.

If you are middle-class and live in a neighborhood without massive factories, highways, and other sources of noise, odors, and pollution, then entering Elizabethport can shake you up. Not only is it one of the poorest places in this affluent state, but it is surrounded by more massive signs of our urban-industrial machine society than any other place I have studied in New Jersey. The New Jersey Turnpike, the most heavily trafficked road in the United States, is the western border of

Elizabethport and is about one-half mile from Reverend Garlic's ministry. The turnpike is a formidable physical barrier, twelve lanes wide, rising more than fifty feet above the ground, and topped by noise barriers. Only a few roads pass underneath the turnpike and permit access to Elizabethport. Driving into Elizabethport under the turnpike through one of these tunnels makes me feel claustrophobic.

Two massive natural-gas tanks lie about a mile south of Elizabethport and form the southern boundary. The tanks tower over houses located directly across a narrow street and cast a large shadow over them. When we walked around the area in 1993, it was a hot summer day, and the hair on my arms bristled when I approached the fence surrounding the gas-tank complex, probably from the heat.

Just south of the gas tanks, about a mile from the ministry, is the site of the former Chemical Control Corporation's hazardous-waste incinerator. The site neither smells nor is visible to residents. Nevertheless, anyone who has lived in the area for a decade or more should have mental scars. Chemical Control made national headlines when it exploded in 1980, sending flames hundreds of feet into the air and threatening the adjacent gas tanks, the ramps to the Goethals Bridge, and the people of Elizabeth. Journalist Michael Brown described the scene in his book *Laying Waste*: "330-foot mushroom cloud with a brilliant fireball at its epicenter . . . bursting like Independence Day mortars, into colorful cascades."[1] The adjacent Elizabeth River turned a blood-red color as a massive variety of materials, including acids, bases, arsenic, cyanide, flammable solvents, polychlorinated biphenyls, compressed gases, biological agents, shock-sensitive chemicals, pyrophoric materials, and acids, flowed from the site. The front cover of the June 1980 issue of the U.S. Environmental Protection Agency's *EPA Journal* was a picture of the Chemical Control fireball. In December 1993, the Chemical Control cleanup was completed by the federal government at a cost of about $41 million. The 2.2–acre site is now surrounded by an eight-foot-high chain link fence. Contaminated soils are trapped within the site, covered by an impermeable cap and three feet of crushed stone. It is not an exaggeration to say that Elizabethport could have been destroyed by the inferno.

The Bayway petrochemical complex is just south of the Chemical Control site and about one and a half miles from Reverend Garlic's ministry. Owned by Tosco, Inc., Bayway is the largest petrochemical complex on the east coast of the United States. According to toxic-release inventory data supplied under federal regulations, the Bayway facility is the seventh largest waste-producing site and the eighth largest emitter of toxins in New Jersey. Its oil-based and sulfur-based waste products are treated before release. But sometimes there are odor problems and accidents that have sent workers to the hospital.

Overall, the refinery, massive gas tanks, hazardous-waste site, and New Jersey Turnpike are reminders to residents that poor neighborhoods like Elizabethport end up with the obnoxious land uses that suburban Americans do not want in their neighborhoods. That is, NIMBY, or the Not In My Back Yard outcry by suburban residents, often leads to PEPPBY: Put Everything In Powerless People's Back Yards.

A few blocks east of the ministry are Newark Bay and the Arthur Kill. The Arthur Kill is a slow-moving estuary that has a great deal of petroleum tanker traffic. According to data collected by my colleague ecologist Joanna Burger, the sediments of the Arthur Kill have among the highest concentrations of hydrocarbons of any water body in the world. The New Jersey Department of Environmental Protection has started a program to communicate to the residents of Elizabethport that the fish they catch there may be hazardous to their health.

The northern direction sends even more powerful messages to me than do the massive wall to the west, the industries and waste sites to the south, and the polluted water body to the east. On a clear day, New York's World Trade Center, whose twin towers are symbols of elegant economic power, is visible directly to the northeast, less than ten miles away. But to the northwest lies the glide path into New Jersey's Newark airport. All the air traffic passes directly over Reverend Garlic's neighborhood, located about a mile away from the end of the runway. With an average of 1,255 flights a day, Newark is the tenth most heavily used airport in the United States. When a slow-climbing jumbo jet flies over, the sound on the ground is deafening. On the ground, I felt as if I needed to hold onto something to keep my balance. Conversing with residents is impossible when the jumbo jets fly.

Elizabethport contains other manufacturing facilities and businesses, and railroad lines surround and cross the neighborhood. Clusters of abandoned housing, some streets badly in need of repair, numerous littered lots, locks on mailboxes, and beware-of-dog warning signs are symbols of a perilous environment. Overall, Elizabethport epitomizes the multiple problems faced by industrialized, central-city American neighborhoods in the 1990s—that is, massive technological hazards, blight, crime, and a mix of relatively poor people densely packed together.

In July 1993, we surveyed sixty-one residents of Elizabethport. None rated their neighborhood quality as "excellent," and only 26 percent rated it as "good." Thirty-one percent rated Elizabethport as of "fair" quality, and 43 percent rated it as of "poor" quality. This compares to 33, 55, 10, and 3 percent of New Jersey residents who rated the quality of their neighborhoods as excellent, good, fair, and poor, respectively. In other words, these residents of Elizabethport were almost six times (74 percent compared to 13 percent) as likely to rate their neighborhood as of poor or fair quality than were residents of New Jersey as a whole willing to rate their neighborhoods.

When asked which, if any, problems caused them to want to leave their neighborhood, airplane noise and crime were identified by almost 60 percent of the respondents. Motor vehicle noise and heavy traffic, litter or trash, odors and smoke, abandoned housing, occupied buildings in poor or dangerous condition, recreational facilities that attract rowdy people, chemical plants, unfriendly neighbors, uncontrolled animals, and other neighborhood characteristics caused more than 20 percent to want to leave. Overall, each of fourteen potentially stressful environmental characteristics caused 20 percent or more of the residents to want to leave their multiple-hazard neighborhood. In comparison, suburban neighborhoods I have studied and those reported in the U.S. Department of Commerce's *American Housing Survey* publications usually do not have a single environmental problem that causes 20 percent of residents to want to leave. In studies of over thirty neighborhoods, only one located adjacent to the trash incinerator, about a mile from Yvonne Carrington's home in Chester, Pennsylvania, had as many stressful characteristics identified by its residents.

The link between behavioral, blight, and technological hazards and neighborhood quality is striking. The greater the number of perceived problems, the greater the likelihood of a poor neighborhood-quality rating. The average respondent in the area who rated his/her neighborhood as good wanted to leave as a result of 1.1 problems. This compares to 3.9 problems among those who rated their neighborhood as fair, and 8.2 who rated it as poor. A middle-age male resident testified to the multiplicity of problems in Elizabethport: "We need to clean up our street. Animals all over the place. Heavy airplane noise, drugs! You name it, this neighborhood has got it."

A Vision of People and Neighborhood

Within one half hour of beginning the interview, I realized how much I was enjoying an interview with a man who admits to not having a grand plan for the future with an accompanying set of quantified objectives. In fact, he doesn't think such an approach would work in this place. "I don't have a plan, a big dream," said Garlic. "I don't think that's the way it works."

What he lacks in specific goals and quantitative objectives that can be monitored, he more than makes up for with as clear a vision of how to build trust and credibility as I have ever heard articulated. The first element of his concept is to build people.

> Garlic: I'm realistic enough to realize that the things that are going to make a difference in this community are the little things that you do, rather than the big things. It's how people are strengthened, how people begin to become involved in the community, how changes come about—the kind of people that make the decisions, the political decisions, and the social decisions.

Rod Spearman articulated the list of people-building activities at the center:

> It's been a haven for people who need a place to come and renew, strengthen themselves, and refresh themselves. We provide everything from day care to a notary. We educate people, we counsel. This is a place for people to have birthday parties for their children and anniversaries, for religious experiences, and just about any other kind of support service.

> Council member Manny Grova Jr.: I've lived down in the port here in Elizabeth all my life. The center used to be a little place for kids to go to. Now, they've added on an extra section. It's a

center for kids, for after-school programs in the area. They offer some job-training programs. They offer tutoring programs. They try to do rehabilitation for kids who are nonviolent offenders. They have a group of kids, the Rangers, that got together as part of the community service they perform. They go out and do clean-ups and try to improve the appearance of the place. So it becomes a nucleus, and the center of the nucleus is Reverend Garlic. He's the one who had the vision to organize this type of program for kids.

Reverend Garlic's second element of building credibility is patience, stability, and honesty.

Garlic: I often tell people that it took us two years before we could really do anything, ten years before we could gain the trust and the credibility so that people would really believe we were sincere about what we were doing, that we are not here just trying to mislead people, make promises that we are not going to keep.

A lot of agencies, a lot of people, who come to the port to do things, have passed on, and gone out of existence. They don't last. One of the things that has happened with a number of agencies is that they have gotten into financial trouble. People get greedy and take the money.

Chuckling, he added:

I'm proud that has not happened here. In addition, my board of directors has worked very hard to plan for the future of the organization. We have a stable agency, that is accountable; we can demonstrate the stability that's needed to go to a funding source and say what we need. We have all our records.

We never go to a funding source or the city and ask for things we don't need. If we need $15,000, we'll say we need $15,000. I wouldn't ask for $20,000, hoping that they would give me $15,000. We've never asked for any breaks from the city, for letting us slide for any kind of code enforcement, any kind of health inspection.

Although he never stated it as one of his principles, it is clear that Reverend Garlic is convinced that deeds must match words.

Garlic: One of the things that I think is important to our success is that we are consistent in our behavior in the community. For example, I can't cross the street any more in the middle of the block. I have to cross at the light. Yes, I can't jaywalk because I tell the kids to cross at the light. If they saw me jaywalk, they'd say, "Reverend, you're crossing in the middle of the street." They're quick to notice things like that.

Consistently being a role model is a major advantage.

Garlic: I can say things to people and they listen because they know who I am, and they know why I'm here. I said to a woman only yesterday—Ms. Jones, I saw her drinking a cup of coffee on the corner—I said, "You're going to have to learn to do things differently. If you work in this community, you're working all the time. This is not a 9–to-5 job. People see you, whatever you do, that's part of your work. Because you're here."

Reverend Garlic's view that he must be a role model is exemplified by the fact that he lives three blocks from his ministry, across the street from a public-housing project. In fact, his entire family is a role model for what every neighborhood needs. While my words cannot capture the love and admiration for his wife and daughters that I see in his face, the words underscore the commitment they have made.

Garlic: My family, it's because of them, my wife and my children, that I'm able to do these kinds of things, because we live here and have agreed that this is a priority. My living here is as much a part of my work here as being at the center. My house has always been full. People come to my house for family counseling. I have aides there. People come by just to say hello. They come by for dinner. When [students] come home from college, they come there. People come to live with us for a while because they can't get along with their parents. Many times we have not gone on vacation because I have to be here during the summer.

Reverend Garlic's family is a model of family values. Hazel Garlic, his wife, is from Virginia.

Hazel Garlic: My first impression of Elizabethport was not positive. I had come from a very different facility in North

Carolina, a sharecroppers' center, run by the United Church of Christ. The sharecroppers were poor but very upbeat. Elizabethport had a dismal look to it. Debris was lying in the street. A good many people seemed beaten down, depressed. I thought, I don't know what we can do. But Joe had high hopes, and he gave that hope to me. I support and believe as much as Joe that what we do to carry out God's will must be outside the structure of the building. That's why we were able to go into a community such as Elizabethport and stay some thirty years. Our original plan was just to stay five years. But each time we talked about leaving, Joe had a new vision.

Joe and Hazel Garlic met while he was working in North Carolina with sharecroppers. In North Carolina, Hazel Garlic was involved in the Christian Education Program. Presently, she runs a senior citizens program for Catholic Community Seniors, focusing on Alzheimer's patients. Obviously proud of his wife's work, Reverend Garlic said, "That's a tough job. You know certain people are fitted for the job. That's my wife. She's right where she belongs."

The Garlics have three daughters. Married with two sons, Valencia, the oldest, is a caseworker supervisor at a social work organization in Newark, New Jersey. Reverend Garlic's description of her needs no enhancement. "She is very supportive of me, just a good daughter," he says. "We are very close family, and we support each other."

He beams with pride as he describes his second daughter, Heidi:

Heidi, she got that name because at birth, we weren't sure she was going to make it. She was born with Turner's disease [a congenital endocrine disorder typically associated with short stature]. But the one thing she had, that she got from her father, was determination. She went to school and graduated. She was a very good student. She went to Kean College, but at the beginning of her third year, she started to lose her sight. So she had to drop out of school. She's a survivor. She'll be all right. She's taught us a lot of things about surviving. She had a pretty rough time going through school because she is different. It makes us aware of how badly we often treat people who are developmentally disabled. I know it has made me more aware of how to treat people who are different.

And then I have a third daughter, Krishna, who's fulfilling one of my dreams. She's in her third year of law school.

He smiled, and then noted that Krishna would like to become mayor of Elizabeth.

Accomplishments

During Reverend Garlic's thirty-year tenure, the Presbyterian Center has received public notoriety, awards, and mass media coverage for many of its programs.

PROGRAMS FOR YOUTH

The day care center was one of the first things that we started when we came here, because there was a need for it. Our day care teacher was the first person to be hired. I substituted at times, but we needed our own teacher, and we did hire a teacher.

Reverend Garlic explained that his ministry is also responsible for a day care program in Plainfield, New Jersey, also located in Union County.

About ten years after setting up this ministry, they started one in Plainfield. It got into some financial trouble and is no longer in existence, except for the day care program. We stepped in and picked that up. We have about one hundred day-care children and a staff of fifteen.

A related project was working with the youth and young people, just beginning to talk to them, have group activities for them, send them away to camp, help them find jobs, with counseling, to provide another outlet for them to go to. By changing the attitudes of kids who live there, and by placing them in contact with another way of life so they can see all the good things that are going on out there, they will become a part of the inner-city solution rather than a part of the problem. These kids need all the support they can get to stay out of trouble and stay in school. They must also be taught how to make intelligent decisions about their own lives. We hold weekly meetings where films are shown, and speakers come to discuss the problems facing these kids in the dangerous neighborhoods as well as their own homes.

BRAND NEW DAY

Brand New Day is the center's organization for rebuilding housing.

Garlic: The housing is not something that just happened. I did not wake up all of a sudden and say we were going to do housing. It was a process, a slow process. My board of directors and I have always been concerned over what we can do, what kind of strengths we can bring to the community that would last, say, after the Presbyterian Center decided that we could no longer fund it. What could we leave here?

The first thing we agreed upon was that we would always try to strengthen the people who worked here—the staff, the families, and others. But one of the things that kept coming into the discussion, as we talked to community members and others, was the idea of housing. There was just not enough decent housing for people to live in, other than the projects. A lot of people did not want to live in the projects.

Brand New Day was not our first effort. In the 1970s, there was a group that I hoped to form with some banks, the Urban League, and some other people, called HOME: Home Ownership Movement Elizabeth bank. At that time they had a Title IV(a) program that built new homes for families to help families get started as homeowners. As time went on, things got tight at the banks, and they gave us less and less support. That effort faded away.

Reverend Garlic claims that all his training was in the ministry and that he wishes he had had more education. "I was not trained to come in here to do this," he says. "I've had to learn so much. I was supposed to be trained to be a minister, they gave me a theological education." Yet, the more we talked, the more it became clear that he has managed to learn whatever was needed to make things happen. For example,

Garlic: When I talk about banks, there are two kinds of support we need. There is administrative support, and there is support for the agency itself. The banks never stopped supporting housing projects and giving money for loans to families. They stopped the administrative support, and that's the most difficult money to raise.

He explained how this need for administrative support was overcome.

> Garlic: When we formed Brand New Day, the State of New Jersey was coming out with a program through the Department of Community Affairs to provide grants to help agencies develop the capability of building low-income housing in urban areas. They were ready to give out grants, and we were ready to take them. So Brand New Day has not had to struggle. It gave us the ability to hire a full-time director, and that director has been able to develop funding.

When asked what he meant by "ready to take grants," Reverend Garlic pointed to stability and trust.

> Garlic: It matters whether they know you or not. As I got better known in the state, in the Department of Community Affairs, as they dealt with us in the homes, as we did some things, we had a state grant, they gained confidence in us. The same way with the banks. They want to know that you're going to be here, that you're sincere. We can point to the track record of the center and say, "We've been here twenty years, we're not going anywhere."
>
> We had an account with Summit Bank. I had a long relationship with the president. He was a nice guy. He had social concern. He had been on the HOME. So we made an application for a loan. We went through the channels to the loan officer. He nixed it. So one afternoon I got in the car and we drove to Summit Bank. I asked to see the president. And I told him that we wanted this project, and that the center was behind it, and that the center wasn't going anywhere, and I wasn't going anywhere. We needed this to start, and I'd appreciate it if he would help us out. He did.

Using the initial loan as seed money, the center involved other banks. "We wanted to see more banks involved," says Garlic. "For the second project, we got a different bank. City Federal. From there we went to United Jersey, Core States. Other banks have been involved since then. But that first success was key."

I asked if he worried about outsiders trying to exert control over the center and the neighborhood through funding.

> Garlic: Money and other assistance from the outside aren't going to change these poor neighborhoods. Meaningful changes in the poor neighborhoods must come from the inside. But dependable outside support is critical to the efforts.

In 1985, Brand New Day opened its first housing project, a twelve-tenant apartment house in a renovated building on First Street. Jay Bloom, a retired real estate lawyer, was hired as executive director. In 1991, Brand New Day opened a second twelve-unit development in a renovated three-story brick building at First Street and Magnolia Avenue. Reverend Garlic was quoted in the *Star-Ledger:* "There is some hope for the people of Elizabethport. I would like to see the city, private business and banks come together to do this again and again." John Connolly, president of National State Bank, which funded the project, remarked: "We're committed to this area down here. A lot of good things have happened in this neighborhood over the last two or three years."[2] In 1992–93, Brand New Day opened thirteen two-family homes on First Street. In 1995, it opened newly constructed, rather than renovated, housing for twelve families in a three-story building on First Street. This was the first new multifamily housing to be built in Elizabethport in thirty-five years. The *Star Ledger* commemorated the groundbreaking with a story that featured the comments of people who attended it. Mayor Christian Bollwage said: "We need the vision of Brand New Day to provide the best we can for the citizens of Elizabeth. I commend Reverend Garlic for his vision, foresight and determination with the project." Al Faella, neighborhood services director, praised Brand New Day for being special: "You just can't build buildings, you must build neighborhoods, as well, which will lead to better communities."[3] In 1996 Brand New Day began negotiating with the City of Elizabeth to purchase land for the construction of seven townhouse buildings to house forty-eight families. On May 5, 1996, the *Star Ledger* discussed the opening of the latest set of Brand New Day units. Councilman Manny Grova, who represents the port area, said:

"In 1985, a Brand New Day came to Elizabeth and that new day was bright. Every year that a new project is created that new day becomes brighter."[4]

COMMUNITY PRIDE DAY

Reverend Garlic expressed distress at the negative reputation the neighborhood had acquired, and how that negative perception was a burden on the children and families. In 1990 the Presbyterian Center sponsored the first Community Pride Day for Elizabethport with a parade and picnics. In 1991, a second Community Pride Day was held. The community presented honors to people who had made contributions to the neighborhood. Reverend Garlic, who organized the activity, said, "All of those who [were] honored exemplify outstanding commitment to others. They have made Elizabethport a good place to live." For example, Anna Jackson was honored as a long-time community leader and founding member of Helping Hands, a part of the Presbyterian Center. Helping Hands provides emergency housing, food, and clothing for needy residents. Garlic said: "Jackson demonstrates spirit and endurance, despite personal adversities. She has not had an easy life, [she was eighty-seven years old when she received the award], but she's still able to carry on and remain young in spirit." John Riley, owner of the Pioneer Pharmacy, a long-time community business, was honored. According to Garlic, "he was a resident of this neighborhood for more than twenty years and is committed to the need for community health services. He is a man of patience and giving. He takes the time to give back to the community. He's someone we should be proud of. He hires people from our community, which helps a lot of residents get a college education." Bertha Dey, president of the Pioneer Homes tenants' association (public housing) was described by Reverend Garlic as "committed to making things better for the tenant. She has taken on the housing authority and has refused to give in to bureaucrats." Rebecca Pastrana, family counselor for the Proceed social agency, which serves Hispanic families, is known in the community as "madrina," or godmother of our youth.[5]

Reverend Garlic had high praise for people who organize programs for the youth and emphasize community pride.

Garlic: People in this neighborhood don't have cars. They don't get out of this community much, the adults as well as the children. So they need the opportunity to express themselves at times, to have a good time. The Spanish people have a lot of programs in the park.

Establishing community pride sometimes has meant confronting those who are too critical of the neighborhood.

Garlic: The *Elizabeth Daily Journal* had a clip on the front of their paper of a guy who they claimed was the big drug dealer down here. They continued to have this picture even after the guy was in jail. They continued to carry his picture in the paper. I looked at it and said, "This has got to stop." So I went to see the editor, and I said, "Is it so important that you sell papers, that you would continue to have his picture?" So they took it off. This is one of the things I could not have done if he didn't know who I was.

Neighborhood Quality and Change

Reverend Garlic's sense of the neighborhood demonstrates the kind of patience and understanding that the numbers collected in my quantitative surveys cannot capture. He acknowledges many of the problems but feels that the neighborhood is improving, and he includes the public-housing projects in that claim. Garlic focuses on the drug problem:

When I first came here, the neighborhood was stagnant, nothing was happening. Then, things began to get worse. Particularly in the late 1980s, with the introduction of crack cocaine into the neighborhood. Elizabeth became notorious for its drug problems. Elizabeth suffered a pretty bad image. But since that time, I think the community is improving. The drug problem has gotten a lot better. I'm not trying to imply that it's good, because it is still bad. But it's a lot better than it was. The neighborhood is improving. Nobody's moving in, not too many people are moving out. It's just that there are signs of life, things that are happening, there's a little bit more of a positive outlook on things than before.

Asked to explain why the neighborhood is improving, he gives an explanation consistent with his focus on the "us" rather than the "me" approach.

> Garlic: One important thing that happened is the political scene changed. And the police department changed with that. There was the advent of community policing. I think that really helped the neighborhood. Policemen are working to try to solve the drug problem rather than just crack heads and lock up people. The police department used to be terrible here. Police would ride through the community at any time and just lock up people. This was hostile, It was a bad place to live.

Reverend Garlic also praised the local ward councilpersons for having a real presence in the neighborhood.

> Garlic: When I came here, the two councilpersons were invisible. If you would ask, 50 percent, 60 percent, of the people in the community, they probably wouldn't even know their names. You never saw them. You never heard about them. They were just councilpersons that you would see around election time. They never did anything. But the two people we have now have been very active. They've done clean-up projects. They've done other kinds of things, with the homeless, with groups in the community.

Regarding drug dealers, he attributes the reduction of the problem to the community police and tenants associations, and the willingness of active people to make their presence felt in the projects.

> Garlic: We've done some things to try to eliminate some drug dealing. For instance, a group of ministers, not all of them, but some of us, from time to time will take a walk through the projects just to talk to the people there about their problems and to ask them to express their feelings. We ask the drug dealers to move along when they're standing around.

Reverend Garlic is much less concerned about the numerous objectionable land uses that surround the neighborhood. For example, regarding jet noise, his historical perspective places the present problem in context.

Garlic: When I first came here, there was concern by the people in the area, and it was because there were a lot more planes going over. There are a lot less planes flying low over the neighborhood now. But the airport has really worked hard to reroute some of the planes out over the water. They bank hard left now.

While praising the Port Authority for its efforts to reduce the noise problem, he acknowledges that pollution has hurt neighborhood redevelopment and that he and others have engaged in efforts to reduce the problem.

Garlic: [For example,] the city had cleared a lot of land. They tore down a lot of housing, and promised that they were going to rebuild housing. Once the housing was torn down, the city began to stall. One of the major reasons they said for stalling was the noise pollution from the airplanes. And so one of the ways to move that project was to object to them coming over and to try to get the airport to reroute planes. I did participate in some of the activity with other groups. We had several meetings with the airport people, and the Federal Aviation Administration, to talk about that problem at that time.

Our tape of the meeting with Reverend Garlic has nineteen breaks in the transcript because of airplane overflights. But ever the patient realist, Reverend Garlic recognizes that the airport is not going to go away, that the Port Authority of New Jersey and New York has made efforts to reduce the noise, including rerouting planes and soundproofing some of the buildings. Half a cup is better than an empty cup.

Assessment

A week before our interview, Reverend Garlic told his board that he would retire in 1998. It was a propitious time to discuss his assessment of his accomplishments and future priorities, as well as to compare his assessment with those of other prominent residents of Elizabeth.

ACCOMPLISHMENTS

Garlic: I'm most proud of the fact that we are still here. I think because we've been able to stay here, and survive, I'm very proud of that fact.

Rod Spearman: Longevity. The doors have been open. They've never closed. The buildings around us have changed. Businesses come and go. Organizations have come and gone. But we have been here. And that shows that the people trust us. It shows that we've been striving to do what is right.

Sister Jacinta: The Presbyterian Center has always been there in Elizabethport, in the midst of a lot of problems, in the midst of difficult times, and it's always been a place of hope for people. A place where people could go and feel safe. It's offered real stability to the community.

Whenever an established leader retires, there is always the chance that the organization will change, perhaps even fail, and that the facility will close. I told Reverend Garlic that this was one of my major concerns about community organizations headed by dynamic leaders. Reverend Garlic smiled as he gave the following response.

Garlic: The thirty-year project of the presbytery is something that they're committed to. Most of the staff are people who could carry on. But we're going to go through the process of picking a director. I will have some input into that.

In other words, he is convinced that the center will continue after he retires.

Helping children is clearly an accomplishment.

Garlic: A lot of the people who came through the center, a lot of the kids, are today somewhat successful. That we've had an opportunity to touch their lives in some meaningful way. It's made a difference. Two months ago, I had a call from a guy in Atlanta, who said: "I was in a group back in the year—, and I've never forgotten what that meant to me." And we've had people who are still here in the community doing other kinds of things, in the port, in the city, in the school system. It gives me a good feeling. It also makes you want to work harder. But then, you think about the people you lose too. Either they are dead, or in jail because of drugs, or AIDS, or some of the other things that happen around here.

Reverend Garlic clearly has a close relationship with Rod Spearman and uses Rod's wife as an illustration of success.

Garlic: She was real good. You work with young people in cycles. As they come along, some groups are very active, very self-motivated, very positive. She happened to be in a group that came along together, that was active and positive, willing to do things, going places. A lot of good people, who made advancements, such as, as doctors, lawyers, engineers, school teachers, people going into business, writers.

It is clear that the day care, Brand New Day, and Pride Day programs are not an end in themselves but a means toward planting seeds of hope, building people.

Manny Grova: I know many kids who have come through the center and have grown to become good citizens as a result of the help they've received.

Sister Jacinta: The center helped a lot of those kids get into college, and really be able to change their lives, to do something with their lives.

Councilwoman Perkins-Auguste, the first African American councilwoman in Elizabeth, was one of those children: "The center was very helpful to me in 1980, providing me a scholarship so I could go away to school."

PRIORITIES

Elizabethport has so many disadvantages compared to other neighborhoods that I had allocated a great deal of time to focus on future priorities. Consequently, I expected a lengthy list. I got a short one.

Garlic: Something needs to be done about employment. Unless people get employment in some way, this community is always going to be going in the wrong direction.

Reverend Garlic addressed employment from the national, inner-city, and Elizabethport perspectives.

We [the United States] always view employment as a full-time, forty-hour-a-week job, working at some specific place. For a lot of people, that is just not realistic. I think that if a person wants to work two days a week, or if he can only handle two days a week, then they ought to be allowed to work two days a week, or three days a week. That's one of the things I think is going to have to change in the country, I really do. A lot of unemployed people, for instance, who have children, who could work twenty hours a week or twenty-five hours a week, they could come off welfare.

Reverend Garlic points both to a lack of jobs and insufficient public transportation in many inner cities.

Garlic: Whereas at one time there was lot of work for individuals to unload ships [at the port], today they do that with automation, and so much more quickly. [In this area], Union County was so production oriented, and because those jobs are quickly disappearing, Union County is really suffering in employment. [In 1947, there were 17,200 manufacturing jobs in Elizabeth; in 1992, there were 7,100.] For what we're producing, there's limited or no demand. So we have to retool for a service-oriented society. The jobs today are in service, in malls, and those fast-food places. The biggest [corollary] problem, not an insurmountable one, with more jobs, is transportation to where the jobs are. Low-income families don't have cars. That's one of the things we're working on. We have to have public transportation. There are buses there, but not as regular as they should be. Until there is enough trade for the bus company, there are not going to be enough buses.

Reverend Garlic notes some progress that he feels will eventually pay off in jobs for local residents in the adjacent retail development built by IKEA, a large Swedish retailer, just north of Elizabethport and east of the airport.

Garlic: One of the things we did, about three years ago, was to start an employment group. We had a gentleman on the staff here who was a job developer. Their job developer, a job developer from the Social Service Center, and a job developer from the county met. They talked about jobs at IKEA and about the new mall, and how we could work together. We're moving in the right direction.

Jobs, he emphasizes, are a means to his bottom line—building people.

Garlic: The real problem is not drugs. The real problem is that people don't have the opportunity to be creative, to develop, to have any creative work, to be fulfilled. They find other ways to do it. We focus on drugs. We need to spend our time helping people to be strong. Strengthening the family, individuals. Doing things that help people survive. We're caught up in that. That's in front of us. We can do something about that. But it's hard, and it will take time, and we must proceed step by step.

LESSONS LEARNED

Our final point of discussion was lessons that Garlic had learned from his three decades at the Elizabethport ministry and that could be applied elsewhere. The news media are increasingly full of stories about efforts initiated by religious and ecumenical bodies to stabilize inner-city neighborhoods. These range from individual efforts in adjacent towns like Newark and Perth Amboy, to widely publicized efforts in Los Angeles, Miami, New York City, and San Antonio. There is also Habitat for Humanity. I asked Reverend Garlic what strategies and approaches in Elizabeth would be valuable to others. His response was: "I don't think I've done anything out of the ordinary. I think it could be done more effectively than I've done it."

Others we interviewed had a different opinion. Mayor J. Christian Bollwage focused on the facts that the center's efforts are not motivated by profit, that the center makes sure that the facilities are kept up, and that a success like Brand New Day can help other neighborhoods in the same city.

Bollwage: Every so often someone can make a difference in a community. Few people are willing to invest their time and resources in rejuvenating their neighborhood. Reverend Garlic does. It's not the city that's responsible for the success and rejuvenation of Port Elizabeth. We have been a partner in this process. Reverend Garlic is clearly the lightning rod of success in the area. The greatness of the Elizabethport Presbyterian Center is that the members are the ones that are delivering benefits to the surrounding community. They don't come together for their own individual pats-on-the-back. There is no real self-motivation, except to benefit the surroundings of where we live and work.

Brand New Day, under the direction of Reverend Garlic, has been instrumental in attracting state grants for affordable housing projects and has achieved numerous cooperative agreements with the Whitman (governor of New Jersey) administration. He has an organization that is able to monitor the apartments once they're constructed. The units are cleaned; safety is maintained inside the buildings. These actions increase investment. Because of the success of Reverend Garlic, other developers and builders are able to go after other grant money and stimulate other neighborhoods [in Elizabeth] in creating safe and affordable housing. The City of Elizabeth doesn't have the resources or the expertise to build the houses. We're not in that business. But Reverend Garlic is adept at working with the technical and political skills of an administration in both Trenton [the state government] and Elizabeth, in order to benefit his community.

Council member Manny Grova Jr. talked about the need to combine creativity and persistence in stressed neighborhoods:

A lot of the people at the center are from the area. So they know these kids, they know these kids' parents, they know everybody. That's very important. Reverend Garlic, he's the one who had the vision to organize this type of program for kids this way. Another concept he had was to create this Pride Day parade. We're in what's considered the poorest area of Elizabeth. But just because we're poor doesn't mean we can't have pride in our community. And that was something he thought of.

Joe Garlic is not a man of many words. He's persistent, he quietly coordinates everything. There's Brand New Day, that was his vision. He went out and quietly got the people. It's nice to see a vision become a reality; and the only way it becomes a reality is if you have people like Joe Garlic pushing it forward and making it happen. It's nice to have dreams, but if you're not a person to push for them you're not a leader.

Sister Jacinta Fernandes spoke of the Garlic family's commitment as a message to the community:

Fernandes: I've known Joe from the beginning, and the Presbyterian Center, and have been very closely connected with it. I think the key lesson is commitment. I think Joe Garlic was very committed to the people of Elizabethport, doing something to help the people. I think a real sign of his commitment and his family's commitment is the fact that they also live in the area. Joe and Hazel made a decision, a very deliberate decision, to buy a home in Elizabethport so that they could live among the people they served.

Hazel Garlic: God directed us here. I don't think we could have stayed if we did not have the commitment we had from our belief that God wanted us to stay. Joe never did things for himself, always for the community, especially for the children. He was molded by God to deliver a special message for Him outside the church.

Rod Spearman, Reverend Garlic's long-time colleague, appropriately had the final word:

He always had a vision that others may not have had. He has always had a vision of people rising above where they are at. Second, he and his family committed to living in Elizabethport. He could have easily left here and gone somewhere else, and made a lot more money, and had an easier lifestyle. And he didn't. That makes a difference because most people involved in communities don't live in them. If they don't live in the community, they can't really identify with the community on a twenty-four-hour basis. Third, he has a very sharp mind in terms of money management and budgets, as well as understanding that he needed to secure and get quality people on the board, people that were willing to say to him or anyone else, "No, we shouldn't do this, or yes we should do this." Finally, he really genuinely cares about people succeeding and being successful. You take his character, and you see the same character that Christ would want for all of us.

Chapter 4

Neah Bay:
Forward to the Past

Figure 3. David and Jennifer Knowlton, walking to Cape Flattery, Neah Bay, in the northwest corner of the continental United States. *Photo taken by Michael Greenberg.*

MY WIFE, GWEN, and I approached the turnoff on Highway 112 on the way to David and Jennifer Knowlton's house. To the left was the Makah (pronounced 'muh-KAW') cultural center, filled with a long-house, longboats, harpoons, whale bones, and dioramas of the Makah culture. In front of us, the town seemed to fit uncomfortably between the dark green mountains and the soft blue waters of the Strait of Juan de Fuca. The town looks like an intrusion in all this beauty, the flip side of Central Park in Manhattan. I stretched my neck to see the new breakwater and marina. Vancouver Island was visible on the other side of the strait, but I couldn't see the breakwater. Too bad. Maybe I could walk over there later. Driving by the U.S. Coast Guard station, I saw a large black tanker crawling across the strait, probably on its way to Seattle. How utterly dull it was compared to the soft blueness of the water.

A few seconds later we were at the cul-de-sac where the medical personnel of the Indian Health Service live. We parked next to the dumpster. I got out to stretch after four and one-half hours worth of accumulated aches from our ride from Seattle and bumped my elbow against the dumpster. Funny, I thought, the dumpster was the first thing I had seen on this reservation that reminded me of urban America.

I told myself not to let the raw beauty of Neah Bay fool me. Neah Bay is a tough place to live. The community confronts problems that are as difficult to solve as those faced in Chester, Trenton, and Detroit. And because Neah Bay is remote, the problems don't get noticed as readily. David and Jennifer Knowlton, a doctor and a lawyer from main-stream America who have worked and lived in Neah Bay for four years, know the problems of Neah Bay and isolated communities well.

Finding Neah Bay: The Indian Health Service

David Knowlton could be a poster physician for the Indian Health Service (IHS). Certainly, he is the antithesis of Joel Fleischman, the television doctor on "Northern Exposure," who regarded living in a remote Alaskan village as purgatory on Earth. David Knowlton, a Quaker, epitomizes the Religious Society of Friends' sense of obligation to do work to benefit others. Indeed, Quakers' interactions with American tribes date back to the days of William Penn.

> David: I had been thinking about the Indian Health Service for a while because I always wanted to do need-based care, and I wanted it to be rural. I wanted to be part of a small community. I went to medical school with the intention of being a family physician, to really help people who needed it. I focused on wanting to know people, small-family dynamics, what their lives were about, and being able to integrate that with their

medical care. I guess that's where the idea of being a rural
physician came from. You get to know so much about people
and their lives by living in a rural community.

The Indian Health Service in Neah Bay was David Knowlton's
entrée into rural primary care. In 1798, the U.S. Congress created the
Public Health Service (PHS) to assist sick and disabled seamen. In his
seminal history of the PHS, *Plagues and Politics: The Story of the United
States Public Health Service*, Fitzhugh Mullen notes that health care was
the first mission, and it is the one the PHS has provided to the Makah,
other Indian tribes, and Native Americans since the passage of the
Transfer Act of 1954.[1] The IHS is part of the PHS. In 1955, it assumed
responsibility for American Indians and native Alaskans, who together
now number about 1.5 million. With a budget of about $2 billion, the
IHS employs over eight hundred physicians, about four hundred den-
tists, one hundred physician assistants, and twenty-five hundred nurses
at almost fifty hospitals and hundreds of health centers and village clin-
ics. These health professionals are supported by health administrators,
engineers, medical record keepers, and various other allied-health professionals.

Under IHS administration, Native American mortality and mor-
bidity rates have declined, especially for sentinel indicators such as infant mortality, tuberculosis, and gastroenteritis. The 1995 edition of
Health United States, published by the PHS in 1996, reports the age-
adjusted death rates of American Indians and Alaskan Natives as
slightly lower than for white Americans and much lower than for African Americans.[2] The IHS budget has also permitted the tribes to support badly needed construction of potable water supply systems and
sewage treatment plants. It is also true, however, that per capita expenditures on medical care for American Indians and Native Alaskans
are only about 40 percent of expenditures for the U.S. population as a
whole.

Jennifer Knowlton, a graduate of the University of Michigan and
Ohio State Law School, saw Neah Bay as an opportunity to live where
she could feel the satisfaction of helping people.

Jennifer: My whole family moved to Columbus [Ohio] from
Omaha [Nebraska] following my dad's career move. He's an

attorney by background and made his career in the insurance industry as an investor. My desire to learn about economics comes from my dad. He liked to talk more about technical aspects of finance. My dad would come to Michigan and once a semester talk to economics students and take us all out for beer and snacks and jive about economics. My mom is sort of a philosopher. Any social issue you can think of, she's thought about. She's also a teacher by training. She's very interested in social issues, so we had a lot of dialogue about social issues, growing up in my house. They were both really involved in my education and my views of life.

I had worked on Wall Street and knew that a corporate life-style wasn't personally rewarding for me. I wanted a career where I could help people. I wanted to do things more community-wide. I figured law school was at least going to prepare me for that, whether it be in government work, city planning, or in a firm.

David and Jennifer met in New Jersey and then moved to Ohio.

David: I graduated from medical school in 1990. Jennifer was in New York City working in the financial district and applying to law school. She got into law school [Ohio State], and that decided where we would be for the next three years. I did my residency at a community hospital in Columbus, Ohio.

Jennifer and David both found Neah Bay.

David: We wanted to add as much exposure to different cultures as possible. We wanted to be on the ocean. We wanted to be in the West. We wanted to have a great feeling of adventure. So we got out the map and looked for the reservations that were remote and on the coast. We found this one, and then we came here when I was in my residency for a month as a rotation, just to make sure that everything would work. It felt really good. So we came.

Jennifer's professional fit to Neah Bay was less obvious at first.

Jennifer: We both wanted to come here. The next issue was what I was going to do. My first impression was that this was a little teeny, tiny, town government where there really is no money to hire me. I was really worried that all the jobs that would interest me would be taken. Boy was I wrong. This place is project heaven. The service unit director for the [health] clinic introduced me to members of the tribal organization. I met the general manager at the time who is appointed by the five counsel members. He said, "I've got tons of projects on which I can use an attorney out here. We need to build our relationship with the state governments. We need a liaison-lobbyist-type person. We have some ordinances here that need to be rewritten and updated, so there's all these various legal projects." I felt good. There were many really interesting projects to be done.

Sharing Health Care with the Community

Lieutenant Commander David Knowlton of the IHS walked into a serious personnel problem when he reported to Neah Bay for duty on August 5, 1993.

> David: When we got here, there were two physicians that didn't belong here emotionally or technically. One of them had done an internship in pediatrics and one an internship in obstetrics. They had never completed a residency, but they had a license to practice medicine. They weren't interfacing with the community. They hated being on call, and they were uncomfortable. What bugged me most was that they were uncomfortable with their responsibility, making the decisions they had to make as physicians—whether somebody needs to go somewhere, what to do, to perform procedures, to perform treatments. They weren't willing to accept the expected percentage of bad outcomes that happen even when you do things properly. The clinic had become more of a clearing house of categorizing people and shipping them out rather than an actual place of performance of primary care.
>
> The community was very upset. They were angry. If somebody came in with, say, a hot, red joint, and they wanted something done, instead of getting a joint tap and finding out what was going on, they would ask the patients if they smoke cigarettes, when was their last rectal exam, how was their blood pressure. Then they would give a referral to drive two hours

where they can get treatment. I have no problem with health questions, but that approach was unacceptable in this environment. My approach is to deal with what the patient wants and develop a rapport that I can use to do prevention. My approach has worked. The two doctors were mad at the patients because the patients weren't listening, and the patients were mad at the doctors because the doctors were being paternalistic and were acting like they knew what was best for the patients, although the doctors knew very little about the patients' personal lives and what was and was not feasible.

Our on-call situation got really ugly. It is extremely cost effective, but the burden is on the physicians. The two doctors were upset about their responsibility to do something when a patient really got sick and they were alone with them.

The issue came to a head when the Joint Commission on Accreditation of Health Care Organizations (JAHCO) arrived for a site visit.

David: These physicians told the commission that our after-hours care program was bad and shouldn't be allowed to exist the way it is. The Joint Commission said, "We're not going to accredit you. You have to have nurses on call, X-ray, lab, and pharmacy." Basically, they wanted us to be an emergency room, which would have cost us about a million dollars a year. They weren't going to give us our accreditation, and then these doctors were threatening to stop being on call after hours which, I thought, was completely unrealistic.

These two doctors left after a year. I was here alone for six months, which was very hard, but it was doable. There was no permanent pharmacist at that time either. I pretty much ran the medical portion of the clinic myself. At the same time we increased the number of people we saw, the patient flow increased, the revenue generated increased. Even though I was alone, it was better. The day they left I realized that I was elated. The burden of their negativity was terrible. The release of that burden was such a positive thing that it totally made up for any amount of work or patient responsibility I had. The most difficult problem about being here alone was having to worry about somebody new, a fill-in physician or pharmacist, with the whole situation every Monday morning with a waiting room full of patients. The whole staff and everybody wants to ask me questions. I realized that I was burning out towards the end of six months. People were just coming and going, coming and going. And there would be gaps.

After about six months, we got another doctor. After about another three months, we got the third doctor, and after about another four months we got the pharmacist. We were without a pharmacist for about sixteen months, so we relied on fill-ins.

The joint commission came back and said, "Look. We talked to you guys, we told you what we wanted you to do. Now we're back to see what you did, whether you made it right or not." So I sat down with the woman and said, "There was never a problem. This thing works great, I think it's a model program. I've never been in a situation out here where I wanted back-up and didn't have it. It's the best we can do and it works. No patients have suffered, lots of people have gotten emergency treatment that they really needed." I explained to her that these physicians were uncomfortable and they [the physicians] had hidden agendas. It was their surveyors who were negligent in not realizing this, and they should be better trained to pick that up.

David received a laudatory response.

David: She [the evaluator] said, "Yeah, this is great. You guys are doing fine." She just gave us a couple of helpful suggestions and that was it. We got our accreditation and a year later we went through an actual full-scale survey again. It happens every three years. At that survey we got accreditation with accommodations, 98–percent score. No questions were asked about the after-hours program.

The community, which had been extremely upset with the idea of losing the after-hours program, was pleased.

David: They were angry that there was even any talk about having after-hours care pulled. They thought it [the joint commission's report] was great.

Jennifer jumped in at this point: "Dave isn't pointing out that he received kudos deluxe for his effort." Indeed, David was awarded the

PHS's achievement medal for his work at Neah Bay. I quote a small piece of what John Heinz, director of the Neah Bay Facility for over thirteen years, wrote on January 26, 1997:

> Director Heinz: The Indian Health Service operates the only outpatient medical facility on or near the Makah Indian Reservation. There are few or no real health-care alternatives for seventy-five miles or two hours travel time. Often weather and road conditions preclude patient transport. The IHS medical program must be prepared at all times to do what is necessary to treat routine and stabilize emergency patients. I have had the opportunity to supervise many clinical directors. Because of its rural and remote setting, Neah Bay is an assignment that can challenge medical personnel in many ways. He [Dr. Knowlton] brought a level of maturity and professionalism far beyond his years. It was that stability that was so very crucial to all programs.

Director Heinz illustrated David Knowlton's value as he described the end of the second site visit.

> Heinz: All arguments and justifications were carefully addressed, but to no avail. As the site visit was nearing its end, it was David Knowlton who in his role as clinical director prevailed upon the joint commission official to find a way for IHS to meet the standard. I feel that it was the strong will and sound clinical arguments of David Knowlton that broke the impasse. In the process, he has saved my patients from unnecessary discomfort, injury, or death and has likely designed an emergency medical services system that could serve as a model for counties and other rural communities.

Dr. Knowlton was also nominated for an exceptional capability promotion to commander, one of three that were forwarded by Dr. Michael Trijillo, head of the IHS and assistant surgeon general of the PHS. While no one from IHS received an exceptional capability promotion during that year, excerpts from the nomination submitted by Dr. Trijillo illustrate David's work: "LCDR Knowlton has greatly exceeded expectations of an Officer of his rank and experience and is hereby nominated for an Exceptional Capability Promotion. [He has] improved a rural and remote health-care program during a period of significant and prolonged hardship." The letter focused on his work during the crisis but added: "He has fostered a continuing cooperative climate between the IHS clinic and tribal health programs, public safety programs, and the tribal leadership. He works closely with the community health nurse, local schools, and Head Start. His work with local community members to develop a Hospice Service in Neah Bay has been particularly appreciated by community members."

David is genuinely proud of the clinic and uncomfortable with the accolades. But he has earned every bit of praise. It is rare to find a doctor who has invested so much time in learning about his coworkers and patients. While we walked through the clinic, I was struck by how much he knew about the professional and personal lives of the people he worked with, and how much he relied on that information in his practice. The next day, we attended a birthday party for a young son of two of his colleagues at which the Knowltons interacted with the James family in ways that few mainstream American doctors ever do. David and Jennifer acted and were treated like family members, or at least like very close friends. After the Knowltons announced that they were leaving Neah Bay, the tribe scheduled a going-away party for the Knowltons. David's personal evaluation of his accomplishments was succinct, if not understated.

> David: Mostly what I feel good about is that I feel that I gave
> the clinic back to the people. I'm not a paternalistic white man
> who thinks I know what's best for them.

Ongoing Public Health Issues

I pressed David about his views of the key public health and related issues that need to be tackled in Neah Bay. Several were apparent in David's annual clinical director reports. The clinic treated 20 percent more patients in 1996 than in 1992. David projects a continued linear increase in patients. The present clinic and staff is too small to accommodate the predicted increases, especially as the population ages and needs treatment for chronic diseases. Currently, the clinic serves only Makah. If non-Makah increase in the community because of tourism, the tribe will be under substantial pressure to provide services to non-Makah, which will further overtax the facilities. The challenge to the Makah is how to best use resources in an already resource-constrained, remote environment that is being squeezed tighter during a time when the local economy is expanding. Pointing to a report written by the Northwest Portland Areas Indian Board as evidence, David and Jennifer fear the implications of the federal government's unwillingness to fund increases in the local health-care budget due to inflation, real increases in costs of providing services, and increase in the demand for services. In 1996, the tribe established a Community Health Advisory Board. David and Jennifer applaud this step. The tribe, they feel, not outsiders, should decide tough resource issues.

Beyond ever-present resource concerns, we discussed a variety of sensitive public health issues. David and Jennifer cautioned me to make it clear to the reader that the cultural and geographic contexts of the Makah are not the same as for other tribes. I needed, they said, to make it clear to the reader that tribes have different priorities. To illustrate the point, David discussed drug and alcohol abuse.

> David: This tribe has a drug/alcohol problem. But this reservation does not have near the alcohol problem that people think of or that exists in the Southwest or in many [mainstream] American communities. The main reason for this is this tribe is much more economically viable than the average tribe.
>
> Jennifer: It seems there are more options to meet fundamental needs.
>
> David: Yes, there are more options for people. Even if you don't have a job, you can feed your family with fish. Health care is free and accessible. Health care here is part of the economic health.
>
> Jennifer: Also, this tribal reservation is located on original tribal lands proximate to cultural resources, and so perhaps the tribe has a different response to reservation life.

I remarked that in my walks through the community, the housing looked weather-worn and some housing looked weather beaten. The literature shows that poor housing conditions are associated with public health problems, so I asked about the association of housing and public health.

David: Yes, you've also got a housing problem. But it is not what you expect. There's a housing crowding problem, but it doesn't put people on the street. The climate's relatively gentle. So if you don't have electricity or heat, you're all right. And people heat with woodstoves all the time.

Jennifer: I think, Michael, that the climate is so accommodating. Anthropologists say that what has shaped this tribe through the centuries is that there's so much more art and leisure activities here because the tribe was able to sustain itself. Granted, they didn't choose the most easy method. Whaling is a tough method of sustaining yourself. But the woods are full of elk, the rivers were full of salmon; these folks were not wanting for food or trying to eke out some sort of agricultural lifestyle that's hit and miss. I've read that their cultural richness is dependent on the fact that they had so many resources at their disposal. It continues today. Of course, the climate is still moderate. You can live pretty comfortably in a trailer, and pass it down to your kids.

David: So the kinds of pathologies associated with homelessness that you find in cities and urban areas are rare here.

Jennifer: The tribe is proud of its locally based HUD program, which is responsible for much of the housing development. But overcrowding and problems associated with it are important. It is difficult to fund new construction with private funding because it's all tribal trust property. You can't get a mortgage. Now the banks are figuring out a new way to help. They just launched some new programs. While discussing grant opportunities, Washington Mutual described a new program to me about ways to tweak the law a little bit and their banking policies so that you can get some mortgage support.

Meanwhile, there's always some kind of family member, or the community will find some place for you. Or you end up going to Port Angeles if you can't find a place to live here. People who live here have a purpose for being here. They're connected to the tribe somehow. People aren't homeless in the sense that they are living in the street, but they are homeless in the sense they are living in some pretty stressful circumstances in overburdened households.

David and Jennifer identified teenage pregnancy and especially mental stress as key public health problems in Makah and mainstream society. They also tied these public health problems back to housing and stress on the Makah culture. They pointed out that counseling for these problems at Neah Bay is tough because it is so small: everybody knows everybody else, so maintaining anonymity is difficult. Jennifer added: "The pressures of living near the extended family exacerbates the problem for some people."

Jennifer and David explained how the Makah were working on a solution that fits their culture and this remote location.

> Jennifer: They have a great deal of pride about doing things differently here. Loyalty to the family is strong. They are taking care of everybody. They are hustling all over town, taking care of aging aunties, sister's kids when sister is in trouble. They take care of the needs of the elder parents, whatever needs to be done. Things are done differently here, and people do value their family extensions.
>
> One of the projects that I started working on before I left was a domestic violence program. The judge and the social services folks came to me and said, "You know, we really need help not just in domestic violence but in ways to strengthen families." We created a vision of a family center, a one-stop shop for family services. There was a lot of domestic violence money that seemed to be available, and we were in the process of building a domestic violence comprehensive program that involved tribal law enforcement, the judicial arm, and the victim services folks. They're also trying to break the circle of family violence by providing perpetrator rehab. There's a lot of pressure on these people because of the way the two cultures—the white and the Makah—have interacted and how the local culture has been threatened. There's a lot of pressure within families that is intolerable. In terms of quality of life, there's so much that can be done in giving people relief from just the pains of living in an integrated culture that's been oppressed.
>
> You have to work with the whole person, and I've been thinking that something like this family center is going to do a lot to help us work with the whole person and the whole family. The program is training a Makah to become a domestic violence counselor as well as a cadre of Makah social counselors, social

workers to build this family center. So, yes, it's high-pressure living. At the same time you're talking about a culture that lived in a longhouse with all its extended relatives. This culture has developed tools for handling these stresses before, and they'll do it again. The tools will be different from what you and I have experienced.

Working Together on Emergency Health Services

David and Jennifer shared the experience of working together for the benefit of the community. Whenever I asked a question, I got two responses. Here is one example, an important one for this book, about the provision of emergency health services.

> Jennifer: My first grant-writing project was with Dave's group at the clinic. The tribe was extremely upset: "Oh, no, we're going to lose our after-hours care. What are we going to do?" So they assigned my boss to figure something out. He interviewed people at the clinic. Then Dave's boss called me up and said, "You've got to write this grant." I was pretty worried. I had not written a grant before, and I had two and a half weeks to write it.
>
> I sat down and took a look at it and it was just paperwork. I thought: "Ah, heck, I just had three years of training in paperwork. I know how to do this. Just follow the instructions." I ended up interviewing EMTs and throwing together this grant for back-up emergencies that was really a demonstration project. The problem was timing. I was trying to do in one week grant projects that take a month to do. The support staff will remember. I was going crazy writing grants. It was a very panicky situation. Everyone was panicked, not just me. Dave's boss was, the tribe was. Even the Coast Guard people were worried about losing the after-hours care. When I went to Coast Guard meetings, the wives were extremely agitated.
>
> David: Jennifer's right. The Coast Guard, everybody was freaking out about it, and appropriately so. We needed to increase the basic life-support ambulance to advanced cardiac life support. The EMTs were going to be paramedics, so the person having a heart attack or the injured person could receive advanced life support on their way to the hospital.

Context: *Rural Health in the United States*

The history of rural health in the United States lends credence to the anxiety of Neah Bay's residents about public health services. For most of the late twentieth century, rural health services have been decreasing, not increasing. During the 1930s, the Farm Security Administration (FSA) started providing prepaid health services for low-income farm families. In 1942, the FSA serviced six hundred thousand people in 1,100 rural counties (over one-third of the counties in the United States). In 1946, the Hill-Burton program began investing in the construction of medical facilities. Almost one-half of the investments were in communities with populations of less than ten thousand. This action improved rural health facilities but did not solve the shortage of trained medical personnel.

Rural physician shortages became even more acute in the late 1960s and 1970s. For example, in 1970, urban areas had an average of 192 physicians per 100,000 people, compared to 41 in rural areas. Fifty percent fewer general practitioners were located in rural areas in 1970 than in 1930.[3] In 1990, almost 5 percent (144 of 3,000) of all U.S. counties did not have even a single nonfederal resident physician. A total of 483,000 people lived in those counties in 1992, for an average of 3,300 per county. Some of the counties with no doctors are on the fringe of urban areas, but most are not.

Transport of cases to an emergency-care center in less than one hour reduces mortality by about one-third.[4] So remoteness is a threat, especially during an emergency. During the 1980s, over five hundred rural hospitals closed, and many lost emergency services. When combined with the lack of 911 emergency numbers in some rural areas, lack of equipment, and poor roads, the closing of facilities that can handle emergencies increases the risk for the traumatized. For example, 70 percent of the population lives in urban areas, but 70 percent of trauma fatalities from motor vehicle accidents occur in rural areas.[5] This is partly explained by poor roads, older vehicles, and lack of seat belt use, as well as remoteness.

The national and state governments and private organizations have tried to address this urban/rural imbalance of medical personnel with limited success. The major reasons for the decline of medical personnel and the closing of facilities include declining rural economies, the increasing cost of medical insurance and medical technologies, and the feeling on the part of many medical personnel that a rural life does not offer the same opportunities as an urban one. The Makah, in short, have good reason to be anxious about their public health system.

The Makah, Neah Bay, and Looking to the Past for the Future

I came to Neah Bay to focus on the impact of remoteness on health care, especially emergency services. In addition, the Makah reservation offered the opportunity to explore the interactions of culture, public health, housing, and economy in a context that most Americans don't know. The Makah reservation is located at the northwest tip of the continental United States in Clallam County, Washington. The Pacific Ocean is the western boundary, and the Strait of Juan de Fuca is the northern boundary. Most of the forty-four-square-mile reservation consists of steep mountains and hills with elevations of 500 to 2,000 feet. Views from these peaks are spectacular, as good as the Grand Canyon and the redwood forests. But most of these beautiful slopes exceed 70 percent, which means that they are unstable, subject to severe erosion, and hostile to conventional human settlements. Erosion is enhanced by eighty to one hundred inches of rainfall yearly. The wet, mild weather produces the characteristic lush forest vegetation of the Northwest. The currents also bring mild winters, and the nights are very long during the summer, as I found out when I tried to go to sleep at 10:00 P.M. without pulling down the curtains.

The Makah's lifestyle is suited to their environment. While surrounded by dense, mostly hemlock forests, the Makah have found that the combination of steep slopes, heavy rain, and unstable clay soils makes timber harvesting a dangerous and difficult business. Agriculture for commercial purposes is unfeasible. We saw some cattle grazing in the salt and mud flats behind the beaches. But too many cattle in this environment would destroy the delicate ecosystem.

For all these reasons, the tribe has relied heavily on the coastal waters and streams. The Makah way of life was to move between fishing, hunting, and gathering areas in an annual cycle. Whales were hunted in the fall and spring, seals in the summer, salmon during the summer and fall; shellfish, berries, bark, and roots were gathered at various times. In her 1991 article for *National Geographic*, Maria Parker Pascua explained that Makah, a name given to the tribe by a neighboring tribe, means "generous with food."[6] The Makah people know themselves as Qwidicca-atx (Kwee-ditch-chuh-aht), or "people who live on the cape by the rocks and seagulls." During the negotiations leading to the treaty between the U.S. government and the tribe, the head tribal chief is reported to have said: "I want the sea. That is my country."[7]

The Makah share their environment with other species. For example, I read that upwards of fifty bald eagles inhabit the cedars along the shoreline where salmon are abundant. When we visited the beach, I saw twelve circling over our heads, which is more than I had seen in my entire life. I stared at them for at least ten minutes like a kid who had just walked into a candy store with 5 dollars in his pocket.

The Makah's annual economic cycle was disrupted by the arrival of the Europeans, who brought smallpox, a microbial killer, as well as guns, to challenge the tribe's traditional access to land and the sea. The 1855 treaty between the Makah and the United States took much of the tribal land. The U.S. government promised to provide education and health services and tried to steer the Makah nation into agriculture and forestry.

The sea remains the Makah's economic foundation. Judged by U.S. census data, the environment has not been bountiful. Some of the two thousand Makah are able to rely on the sea and forests, they have health care, and some are happy to pursue part-time employment so that they have time to engage in artistry and seasonal fishing. But about 80 percent of Makah households are in low- to moderately low-income categories according to U.S. census tabulations. Unemployment rates hover around 50 percent and reach over 60 percent during the winter. Jobs are as critical an issue for the Makah as for the people of Elizabeth, New Jersey, and Chester, Pennsylvania.

The Marina: Looking to the Past for the Future

In the 1940s, the federal government built an 8,000–foot-long rubble-mound breakwater to control waves. The breakwater connected Waadah

Island in the Strait of Fuca to the western shore of Neah Bay. Jennifer's main project has been funding the construction of a marina protected by a 1,500–foot-long breakwater built by the U.S. Army Corps of Engineers and located within the 8,000–foot-long breakwater constructed in the 1940s.

> Jennifer: That's the project that's supposed to pretty much shape the economy here for the next fifty years. The tribe had been submitting feasibility studies to the Corps [Army Corps of Engineers] every five years for the last twenty-five to thirty years. By the time I came, five years of environmental permitting and environmental groundwork had been done, and what they needed was the project moneys for construction. The director of economic development for the tribe had researched the funding agencies that needed to be contacted. Suddenly it [the marina] became feasible. Why? It had to be politics. Maybe, this is one of the last navigational projects they'll be doing.

In the early 1990s, the Clinton Administration placed severe restrictions on timber harvesting in the West because of the existence of endangered species. For example, in 1990 it listed the northern spotted owl as an endangered species, forcing the State of Washington to reduce lumbering. For the Makah, the spotted owl controversy was an unexpected opportunity because the administration called upon the federal agencies to stimulate economic growth in stressed areas.

> Jennifer: Teams of federal, state, and regional agencies were set up to help instead of hinder reinventing government. The state had the WACERT (Washington State Economic Revitalization Team), the feds had a team, and there was also a regional component for the northwest tier (called RCERT). I served as a representative from the tribe on the WACERT team.
>   WACERT really made the project click. Our Economic Development Director said: "In order to get, gain access to these folks for timber money, we have to do this WACERT thing. Okay, Jen, you represent the tribe, get in there and figure this out." The general manager held an economic summit and invited some politicians, some on the WACERT. She understood fundraising. She shut the doors and said, "No one's

leaving the room until you can tell us what we are eligible for through your funding agency. You don't have to commit funding, but just tell us what are we eligible for." Someone from WACERT was present and said, "We've already created a process to do what you're asking for. You'll eventually have to submit a grant application to each funder. The process starts with a two-page proposal which explains the project, and then we'll break it down and tell you who to go to for the funding." We were one of the first projects to go through this elaborate process. We had seven funders and nine grants. Actually, eight grants and one loan for $1.2 million through USDA, their rural development agency.

Clearly, President's Clinton's intervention around the spotted owl issue spurred the agencies to work together.

Jennifer: [Later, I would assert that] we are a model project for Indian reservations, for rural communities who are pursuing funding from multiple agencies, because we've done it. We had to recognize that it was a new process, we had to be flexible. Maybe we were successful because this tribe is more patient and persistent than other communities.

The project consisted of building a breakwater that was 1,500 feet long, 56 feet wide, and 16 feet high. In addition, a moorage facility for 200 to 250 boats, floats, access docks, and ramps was planned. Water, electricity, sanitation facilities, sewage pumping, a parking area, road access, and navigation aids were part of the project.

President Clinton's Spotted Owl initiative came along during an economic downturn. Salmon catches had severely declined throughout the early 1990s. Since 70 percent of the tribal population depends upon fishing for some or all of its income, the marina project was critical to raise morale. The economic analyses for the breakwater and marina predicted the creation of 275 jobs: 186 by the marina itself, and 90 in associated tourism and retail. For context, 275 jobs comprise over half of the existing jobs in the community.

Jennifer: The whole project was $8 million: $4 million for the breakwater and $4 million for the floats, piers, and other parts of the marina. We were kind of worried about whether or not we could fund that as a community infrastructure facility. We cast it in that light and it worked.

The actual project took only six months to construct.

Jennifer: Isn't that amazing? After waiting for generations, only six months. They dredged in early autumn, took the dredging material and turned it into a new beach as part of their environmental mitigation project just east of the project. You can see that driving through town. Everyone's out there enjoying the beach. It's been seeded for clams, too. Another tribe gave us the seeds for clams.

The tribe expects it to be successful.

Jennifer: In order to be a solid business it's going to need a suitable business facility. The next phase of the project will be to get the money for building a marina business office.

The proposed facility would replace a temporary unit that sits off the road in front of the marina like a stained tie on a new shirt. The building will contain retail, office, conference, and training spaces, restrooms, and facilities for marina tenants such as a laundry.

Jennifer: Recreational boaters will come in from [Puget] Sound. We have sailboats in there all the time, big beautiful sailboats. We get yachts from Portland, Oregon, and California. [The nearest comparable site is 200 miles south or 75 miles east.] The feasibility studies have us breaking even or even making a hundred thousand dollars in a few years. The real success of the project is not necessarily the revenues of the marina itself. The impact it has on business in the rest of the town is critical. We have created a brand new market. Now we have only two thousand people. We don't have enough of a market to get too many businesses launched to support families. If we get a big influx of people, then we'll get an economic multiplier effect. Marine repair and maintenance will be an important business, as will tourism businesses. We could do a summer taxi service. Someone could do a barber/salon. Someone might even be able to convince a bank to open up either a part-time branch or at least a teller machine. But they've been slow to the draw. Boy, are those people conservative.

David focused on the benefits to local fishermen.

David: The people will be able to do winter fishing; the community members won't be restricted to fishing May through September. These guys can keep their boats at the marina so they can have the income all year round and not have to worry about the boats getting trashed.

Documents prepared for the marina project cite 114 destroyed fishing boats in twenty-one years. During the year prior to the preparation of the report, four boats were destroyed by winds of eighty to one hundred mph and waves that reached twenty feet in height.

Jennifer: Dave raises a key point. Year-round fishing is the immediate goal of the project. The cultural history of this tribe is as mariners. The marina is a culturally compatible development, which was a selling point for funding agencies familiar with development. These sentiments are all part of that paper I wrote about how this is a model project for Native American reservations.

David: Beyond the marina's potential economic benefits, it will make a big difference in terms of the people who live here and have families. We expect it to make it economically, but even if it doesn't, it still can change the quality of life.

Finding a Way to Preserve a Way of Life

The Makah are working on strategies that bring increased economic health without undermining their culture. Some of these strategies involve hard choices.

Jennifer: There is a big controversy about how much tourism is good for the tribe and how to work tourists into the community. The marina is only one example. Cape Flattery has always been a big tourist attraction because it is the northwest corner of the continental United States. It has a beautiful lighthouse out on the island—Tatoosha Island—which is a traditional summer fishing spot for the tribe. You can see whales, seals, and sea lions. [When I visited it, I was amazed to see puffins.] The tribe received multiple grants to design and build the 0.7–mile trail as a tourist attraction.

Cape Flattery has incredible therapeutic beauty; it is fantastic. The trail design turned out better than anyone could have foreseen, and that is because the architect was just great. It was a labor of love. The people in town really enjoy it. They talk about it and talk about it. It's been featured in Seattle papers regularly.

The issue for the tribe is how much tourism and what kinds of tourists to attract.

Jennifer: Outsiders have played a role in the local economy and likely will in the future. They didn't have a major impact on the way people here live because the fishermen were coming in, going to the dock, getting in the boat, going out. They were maybe going to Washburn's General Store. The museum has been here, so it's been attracting tourists too, but they come to the museum, come to the store, and go. There have always been people coming for the trails, like Cape Flattery.

In 1970, a discovery was made at one of the former Makah villages. Five longhouses and over 50,000 artifacts were discovered in excellent condition. These were eventually brought to a museum that was opened in 1979. About fifteen- to twenty thousand visitors a year come to the museum, which includes an incredible outdoor longhouse, made out of hand-split cedar planks, that really gives the feel of communal living conditions.

Jennifer: People come to the museum, come to the store, and go. Now we're actually encouraging and promoting the Cape Flattery Trail and making it easier to use with boardwalks. We're obviously encouraging tourists to bring their boats here and maybe use the services.

The question for the tribe is where to draw the line. How many tourists is too many?

Jennifer: It's not my home, but in terms of having tourists out here, I think tourism can be okay, if it is very controlled. One of the things that keeps this community in balance is the fact that it's insular, that it's remote, and that if you open up access you're just allowing the more negative aspects of development to supersede the positive aspects.

I raised the possibility of setting up a gambling casino and bringing in people by boat from Seattle and Vancouver. Jennifer and David grimaced. Jennifer noted that there is insufficient density for a casino. Furthermore, she doubted that the tribe would permit such an intrusion.

> Jennifer: I guess people do things carefully and slowly around here to see to what degree it will impact the culture. I feel that kind of hesitation in terms of planning projects that could really change the quality of life. These people know that development comes at a cost. People want to understand what will happen before they leap. From what I've seen, this tribe does not want to maximize economic development here. Economic development is just one component of what they're doing here. They have so many other goals. They're trying to develop each person and a nation, not just bank accounts.

Toward this goal, the Makah are perpetually defending the tribe's environment against outsiders who are indifferent to the majestic beauty of Neah Bay.

> Jennifer: This place has been threatened by the cavalier attitude of others.

The Strait of Juan de Fuca is characterized by poor weather, narrow passages, swift currents, and rock islands in the shipping lanes. Climbing to the top of one of the many hills overlooking the bay, Jennifer pointed to spots where ships would routinely stop and discharge their bilge water. On July 22, 1990, the *Tenyo Maru* spilled over 100,000 gallons of oil, which caused considerable damage to the coastline. Jennifer and David have not witnessed any oil spills. While we walked on the beach, where we saw a dozen bald eagles, they told us the story of an impaled cargo ship discharging boxes of expensive running sneakers that washed up on the shore and were subsequently sorted for style and size by local people.

The Makah's livelihood is more likely to be threatened by spills of oil and chemicals than benefited by unplanned free-of-charge sneaker deliveries. The tribe is seeking to develop an oil-spill contingency plan involving the Coast Guard and many others. After years of debate, the U.S. Coast Guard has agreed there is merit in the tribe's plan to station a tugboat near Neah Bay, a precaution that would reduce the spill-response time from an average of six to nine hours to an average of three to four hours. As part of the activities leading up to the construction of the marina, new wastewater and potable water facilities were built, with the tribe playing a major role in planning and evaluating the impact of the options. Jennifer views these environmental-assessment activities as logical and necessary steps the tribe is taking to assume control of its vulnerable environment.

The Knowltons consider improving education as critical to the future of the tribe.

> David: The quality of education really needs improvement. Many don't see any of the real benefits from it, which is another important thing about being out here. Being in the community and being in touch with the children is providing a source, a role model for the things that education can do for you. That's been really important, and we've been told that specifically.

Both Jennifer and David know that long-distance learning is going to help.

> Jennifer: There are outreach programs here. You can get a four-year degree and never leave the reservation. It's extremely expensive to go to college here because you suddenly lose your health care, your housing. You might even lose your place in line for housing if you leave. You'd lose all your family support. This is a remote small town. It's small-town people. Going to the University of Washington is a very disorienting experience. You might need extra schooling too because in high school, even if you were the valedictorian, you might not feel ready for the change in lifestyle. Some students need some remedial training, and they can get that training locally or stay here and get their college degrees. The tribe views this [type of education] positively. If people can get their education, the odds are they will stay here. They're just creating better, stronger, basic human resources. Education empowers the people, and I believe that is what the whole point of the development is.

Next Stop: Eugene, Oregon

The day we arrived for these interviews, June 27, 1997, was David's last day in the clinic. After many months of careful thought, David and Jennifer chose to leave the Makah reservation and move to Eugene, Oregon. David expects to do more direct delivery of medicine and less paperwork and administration.

> David: Family practice. I'm going to start delivering babies again. It's going to be hard, changing from one job to the other. Every day it's just going to be a bombardment of patients and much less administrative stuff, which is what I think I really want.

David swears by the experiences he had at Neah Bay.

> David: This training has been fantastic. I know so much about how a medical clinic functions. I really feel like if I wanted to I could go and start my own clinic somewhere.

To the college students who want to be medical students, David said:

> I'd tell them that if I had this to do all over again, I'd do it. I feel happy that I've been here, that I've done this, that I'm ready to leave. It's an experience that I'm glad to have had, and I would do it again. I've learned more in the past four years about being alive, being a community member, being a healer in addition to a physician, than I think I'd learn anywhere in a lifetime. If you come to a place like this, try to be a part of the community, of people's lives; don't have a paternal attitude. Try and find out who people are and work from there. It's an experience that will last you a lifetime.

Jennifer also thinks her work experience was anything but backwoods.

> Jennifer: I got a really huge education about how tribal organizations are run. Neah Bay has a lot more government here than you'd expect from a mainstream small town. These 2,000 people have the equivalent of federal, state, and local government functions. At first I was scared. But the more I succeeded,

the more I realized what a fantastic experience this place has been.

Jennifer and David entered the formal interviews with a very personal story that demonstrates what is at the heart of the Makah and how the Makah had rubbed off on the Knowltons. In 1996, Jennifer was diagnosed with cancer.

> Jennifer: The chairman of the tribe came as soon as they found out that I was sick. I had to go to chemotherapy every other week, eleven sessions. I kept my job, people brought food and flowers to dry up the tears. The Makah people taught me a lot about how to be sick. In comparison to the Makah, people in mainstream society are not taught to socialize very well. Five-year-old children in this culture are already socialized. At first, it felt intrusive. Everyone knows everything about our lives. But you realize that it is heartfelt, genuine here. These people are incredibly gracious no matter the stress.

The cancer was defeated and Jennifer became pregnant. In May 1997, Benjamin Alexander Knowlton was born. We played with six-week-old bright-eyed Benjamin, a whirlwind of activity and zest for life. In a way, the timing of Benjamin's birth was as improbable and rewarding as finding people like his parents thriving and feeling privileged to have lived in a physical and social environment alien to their previous experiences. Yet juxtapositions of optimistic, confident, ethical, and adventurous people like the Knowltons, with gracious and caring hosts like the Makah have led visionary Americans to support the IHS, the Peace Corps, both domestic and foreign, and other low-budget programs as necessary vaccinations to protect chronically stressed communities that are out of the urban/suburban mainstream.

Ground Zero: Concerned Citizens Fight Against
Chapter 5   Massive Poison Machines

Figure 4. Robert Carson, Ann Parker, and Kerri Blanchard, in the background their nemesis, the incinerator, Rahway, New Jersey. *Photo courtesy of Bill Blanchard.*

GEORGE DAWSON and I park in front of Ann Parker's house. Like a fighter pilot looking for an enemy plane, I quickly glance from side to side, trying to see if the neighborhood has changed. It seems the same as two years ago. Dusk is settling down over the residential street, and it looks and feels quiet, the way a suburban street is supposed to feel during the late summer months. But the softness of the moment is deceiving. I have been on this Rahway street in the morning, when garbage trucks were on it heading toward the Union County incinerator located about three-quarters of a mile to the northeast. It was not soft and quiet then.

A great deal of residual anger exists in this neighborhood. People speak in unflattering tones about many of the prominent elected officials and government organizations. Since I have not interviewed the people being criticized, I have used pseudonyms for them and have sometimes switched gender and age. The characteristics of the three principal local leaders have not been disguised.

Ann Parker greets us at the door. She looks the same as when I saw her last, which was a few years ago at a Rutgers University conference for journalists. Bob Bullard, Ann Parker, and I were each addressing reporters on the subject of environmental racism. Bullard, then a professor from the University of California and a leading spokesperson about environmental racism in the United States, gave a rousing speech. Parker, introduced as a citizen activist, got at least an equal amount of applause for her passionate attack on the County Utilities Authority (CUA), accusing it of environmental racism. A slender, African American woman with a soft, gentle voice, Parker, I imagine, is among those wonderful mothers who read lots of bedtime stories to her children before tucking them under the covers. The image causes me to laugh because this is the same Ann Parker who tore into John Jones, an African American and chair of the CUA, for betraying his race.

> Parker: Does it make you feel good? Does it make you feel
> you've reached the pinnacle of your career? To sit on and head
> the authority that insists on this placement in Rahway is the
> most horrible and unfeeling thing you could ever do.

I remind myself that anger must be a component of street fights against massive technology invasions.

Inside, George and I are introduced to Kerri Blanchard and Robert Carson. Blanchard is a petite woman who looks to be in her early thirties but has teenage children, so she is probably a bit older. Her blond hair and gentle face combine with her youthful appearance to make her seem like someone who would be a member of the PTA (which she is) rather than someone who was arrested for picketing in front of the incinerator site. Kerri Blanchard is as forthright a person as I have ever met. She says what she believes, without hesitation. Raised in Jersey City, she worked on political campaigns for Democrats, against nuclear weapons, and for other agendas which she proudly labels "liberal." When she moved to Rahway at the urging of her sister, she worked as a crossing guard and a prison matron in order to "learn more about the community." She fervently believes in improving cities and preserving the environment.

> Blanchard: I think people should live in the city. I don't agree with people building homes on the seashore, on the edges of the water. They should stay the heck in the city and leave the animals to have some space. I just believe in a firm commitment to the cities and raising the quality of city life.

Rahway, an industrial city of four square miles and about twenty-six thousand people, is a special place to her, and she will fight to keep outsiders from using it as a dumping ground for everything they don't want in their own neighborhoods.

> Blanchard: What a beautiful town. This place is great. I really love it. I think a lot of people who grew up in Rahway just take it for granted. To them there's nothing special about the small-town atmosphere. To them there is nothing special about the river that runs through town. I love the people of Rahway. I like that it's a racially diverse community. I'm not letting these people get away with this.

Robert Carson fits my image of a chemistry teacher probably because he bears a resemblance to my own high school chemistry teacher. Robert is about six feet tall, thin, and scholarly looking, and I imagine him carefully measuring chemicals and instructing students about the intricacies of experimentation. Raised in Brooklyn, he joined the navy as a nineteen-year-old in 1966 to get away from a "tough home situation and to see the world." By 1970, Carson had seen enough in Vietnam.

> Carson: When I joined the navy, I didn't know where Vietnam was. By the time I got out, I couldn't believe what was going on. When I started to find out, I got into all these social movements.

Carson, who moved from Brooklyn to Rahway at the request of his wife, who was raised and wanted to live in Rahway, carried his newly discovered activism across the Verrazano Bridge into Rahway. Carson sounds and acts like an organizer.

> Carson: I [became] involved in labor activity in this area. As a matter of fact, I got kicked out of the union for organizing against the staff.

Superficially, Ann Parker, Kerri Blanchard, and Robert Carson have nothing in common. They are not the same race, sex, or age, and the three activists are different with regard to education, length of residence in the neighborhood, location of residence in the city, place of birth, occupation, and other demographic characteristics that the U.S. Census Bureau and public opinion polls collect. What they have in common is not tabulated by census takers. The trio is furious. They believe that they can influence the course of events, and they are tenacious. Ann Parker characterizes them as "three angry pitbulls."

The Rahway Incinerator

The object of their ire sits next to Route 1, one of the most heavily trafficked roads in New Jersey. Opened in February 1994, the Union County incinerator has a capacity of 1,440 tons of garbage a day, and it cost $280 million to build. Merck's giant pharmaceutical complex and the Rahway state maximum-security prison, popularized in movies, are nearby. Furthermore, an active landfill, a closed landfill, a petroleum storage tank farm, a small airport, a sewage plant, a state motor vehicle inspection station, junkyards, and various other industrial and commercial facilities are within two miles of the neighborhood. Yet the incinerator marks Rahway because its stack and plume of white smoke are visible from the New Jersey Turnpike (more than a mile to the east) and from the Rahway train station (about 1.25 miles to the west). It can't be avoided; it looks like a giant upside-down sledgehammer. Ann Parker and her colleagues see it as a knife stabbed into the back of their town.

In Their Backyard

How did this giant machine end up in the backyard of these street fighters? New Jersey's garbage industry has been portrayed as controlled by organized crime (see, for example, the movie *The Godfather*). During the 1970s, an official investigation by New Jersey's Commission on Investigation concluded that price-gouging monopolies controlled garbage collection and disposal. The state passed laws that imposed two regulatory systems on the industry. The newly formed New Jersey Department of Environmental Protection (NJDEP) was to regulate environmental issues, and the Board of Public Utilities (BPU) was to promote a more competitive system. While criminal activity was the main impetus for the hearings and legislation, the commission was also aware of important changes in the garbage business. Large multistate companies, such as Browning-Ferris, Inc., SCA Services, and eventually Waste Management, Inc., were entering the state and purchasing the small and supposedly corrupt garbage businesses. These multistate companies tended to restrict access to their landfills to affiliated haulers. The BPU forbade that practice. In other words, they forbade flow control.

By the 1980s, concern shifted from price to environmental protection. In 1970, New Jersey had about three hundred landfills. Fifteen years later, about 90 percent of the garbage went to only ten landfills. Federal and state environmental-protection laws had focused attention on protecting ground and surface water supplies and wetlands, and had, in essence, branded landfills as undesirable eyesores that stink and pollute the air and water. In addition, rapid urbanization meant more garbage was generated and more landfill space was needed. When new landfills were proposed, they were invariably declared unsuitable for environmental reasons and strongly opposed by residents.

During the late 1980s, Union County was taking its garbage to three landfills in adjacent Middlesex County. Residents of Middlesex and other counties were angry about being designated repositories for outsiders' garbage. The State of New Jersey responded with a waste-flow plan. Part of it required counties that exported waste to other counties and adjacent states to develop stations at which garbage would be transferred from small to large trucks. Another part required each county to develop facilities for local garbage disposal. For counties like Union, without landfill space, this meant recycling and/or some form of incineration.

Next, State Senator Harry McEnroe steered through legislation that made incineration economically feasible. Counties were empowered to sign twenty-year contracts for the construction and management of incinerators. In order to recognize the unique situations of each county, BPU stopped regulating the fees charged to those who dispose of their garbage at incinerators, so-called "tipping fees." Lastly, BPU permitted builders to spread incinerator construction costs over the life of the projects instead of forcing them to immediately charge the full capital cost to customers. In other words, this legislation eliminated a massive increase in taxes, or the so-called "rate shock."

All of this legislation sent municipal bond investors circling the state in search of places where landfilling was dying. Indeed, some formerly prominent state officials became active in selling bonds. Union County was among the most desperate of the twenty-one New Jersey counties. Its data showed no plausible landfill sites, and recycling was only a partial solution. Union also had among the highest landfilling fees in the United States, and one sensed that it had no control over where its waste would be sent or the cost of sending it. In 1980, the county governing body, the freeholders, proposed a site in Linden, the township just north of Rahway. A nonbinding referendum in Linden was defeated and the proposal was dropped. Stung by the defeat, the county established a utilities authority and hired an advertising firm to recast its message. In 1984, a new proposal was developed to locate a facility in Rahway along Route 1. A 1985 referendum of Rahway voters favored a facility: 55 percent (3,302) to 45 percent (2,731).

Toward Civil Disobedience

Parker, Blanchard, and Carson contend that the residents were tricked into supporting the facility:

> Parker: They changed the wording to make it appear it would give Rahway some benefits, and that it really wasn't bad.
> Carson: It was a real snow job. Right in the text of the referendum it was stated that there would be a reduction in taxes; that Rahway would have control of the traffic; that there would be no environmental impact; that it would be aesthetically pleasing. It didn't mention that it was an incinerator. It said it was a garbage recovery facility.

In 1986, Rahway officials agreed to host the incinerator in return for $1.1 million during the first year of operation, $650,000 for specific community projects, and two seats for Rahway residents on the nine-person Union County Utilities Authority. When asked why their elected officials agreed, Carson showed some sympathy for local officials: "[They] volunteered to put it in Rahway because they probably figured that it would go into Rahway anyway, so they volunteered and tried to control some of it."

Concerned Citizens for the Environment organized to fight the incinerator in 1986.

> Ann Parker: When it was started in 1986, Concerned Citizens was composed only of African Americans, most of whom lived in the vicinity of the proposed incinerator. The Department of Environmental Protection held a public hearing at the Rahway High School when many of our members and a few others spoke about the many dangers that we envisioned if the incinerator were placed here. At the hearing, which was well attended, citizens from all over Rahway were alerted to the possibility of an incinerator in our town. Immediately following that meeting, before we left the building, some of Rahway's Caucasians spoke with us and we decided we should fight this menace together. Residents from nearby towns also joined our group, and the name was then changed to Concerned Citizens of Union County.

The group contacted Madelyn Hoffman, director of the Grassroots Environmental Organization, Inc. Hoffman arranged speakers and workshops for Concerned Citizens. Concerned Citizens was also aided by the Institute for Local Self-Reliance. Under the direction of Neil Seldman, its director, the institute did a study of the county's waste-management plan.

> Carson: It showed that the plan was probably not well planned, because their estimates for garbage were way too high and the financing was not well estimated. The book contained two complete plans, giving us alternatives. One involved an incinerator of a different kind, and one was a nonincineration plan. This was presented to the city government, the county government, and the Union County Utilities Authority. No comment was ever made on this [document].

Rather than being given a chance to defeat the facility using logic, when Concerned Citizens confronted proponents of the facility, "no one was allowed to present the opposing point of view," says Blanchard. "[They] got extremely angry and attacked us personally. They didn't want to hear it. They wouldn't hear it. We got some serious harassment."

The three representatives of Concerned Citizens provided numerous detailed examples of what they consider abuse of power by elected officials and businesses who viewed the incinerator as a "political plum." They charged officials with accepting campaign funds for support of the incinerator. The citizens charged companies with deceiving the county and local population. And they charged officials with conflicts of interest, covering up their misdeeds, and threatening environmental organizations that came to their defense with loss of their tax-exempt status. Concerned Citizens even felt betrayed by a state environmental organization for sacrificing Rahway as part of a deal to get state officials' support for canceling other incinerator projects in New Jersey.

> Carson: There had been a proposal entertained for one in every county. That was ridiculous, and I think they knew it was ridiculous. So they said we would take the four that exist, and we would add two. That was the deal. They sacrificed us.

Local opposition to the facility quickly increased. Some of it was related to environmental issues, specifically air pollution and truck traffic and the fact that the community had a disproportionate number of African Americans.

> Parker: We were concerned about what would be coming out of the stack and from the trucks barreling down our streets. They wanted to put it in a minority neighborhood, and we felt it certainly didn't belong there.

The more we talked about the opposition, the more Parker, Blanchard, and Carson focused on what they consider misuse of political power, greed, and deceit. Concerned Citizens believes that there was a "total denial of the democratic process."

> Parker: We know how wrong this thing is. We know it shouldn't be.
> Blanchard: I just felt very strongly at first that, if the

government understood it was wrong, we could make a difference. I think the idea of burning garbage is just abhorrent to
most people. But afterwards, I got fed up about it. You could see
so clearly the rip-off of it all.

Carson: I think that's what got people so dedicated. If you
look back at the people who did the civil disobedience, and the
people who really put things into the organization when it was
jumping, what you saw was a blatant denial of democracy. It
was a slap in the face. It was local and county government at its
worst. The thing was a fraud. There was no reason to build it.
There was certainly no reason to build it in this neighborhood.
The potential danger from it was just totally ignored. The
alternatives, which would have been much cheaper, and more
beneficial, and more efficient, were just completely ignored.

The vendor showed up with a nice package. They said to
the county executives, "You have a garbage disposal problem.
We have the solution." They gave them a nice song-and-dance
about their incinerator. "It's clean. It's going to keep you out of
landfills. It's going to make you money because you will be able
to sell electricity. You won't have any problems with it. It's
going to be a turnkey project. We'll put it up and give you the
key, and that's it." They got a $16 million loan from the state to
start the planning. And then they started spending a lot of
money on this. They had a few-hundred-million-dollar project
staring them in the face, which is the largest public works
project ever attempted in Union County. Once it was on the
rails, they weren't going to say no. That was exactly what it
was. It was a combination of shortsightedness, people with no
imagination, and people with a vested interest who were
pushing their own agenda.

I cannot verify or deny the accuracy of these assertions about the
incinerator as a political plum. But frankly, I am more interested in Concerned Citizens' reactions and tactics than I am in their perceptions of
what the proponents of the incinerator did. Concerned Citizens hoped
to convince state officials who were running for election that the incinerator was a bad idea. After numerous attempts, they became much
more aggressive.

Parker: We had Mary Stevens, who was on this project like it was her life mission. She really believed that if we spelled it all out, [the candidate] would understand and help us. She pursued this relentlessly. We finally got a meeting with the candidate. We called [the candidate] a hundred times and more. We started appearing at those town hall meetings, when [the candidate] was to appear in public, asking questions about the incinerator. We tried for over two years to get a meeting with [the candidate]. We wound up—this was one of the better actions that we did—following [the candidate] around. Whenever [the candidate] made an appearance, we would pop up, with some kind of crazy, dramatic thing. Kerri got arrested in a town hall meeting.

Regarding the candidate who ran for state office, says Parker, "We got all the election campaign donation records. In 1993, we ran a campaign to dump [the candidate]. We picketed [the candidate's] house and almost got arrested."

Concerned Citizens was able to organize demonstrations attended by over 300 people. As many as fifteen people, including the three activists, were arrested. The incinerator site was the place of many demonstrations. But people's homes were also picketed.

Blanchard: If [the government official] is going to destroy our homes, what are we going to do—sit back and give him the benefit of his sanctuary while he comes in with these heavy-booted politicians, and just destroys our town?

While not comfortable with civil disobedience at first, Carson noted that "it was amazing, the number of groups like ours, all over the place. Sometimes you think, my God, there must have been a majority of the population who has been in active opposition to their government at a very local level at one time or another."

Concerned Citizens was unable to stop the incinerator from opening, and it remains open.

Carson: We think with all the effort that we've put out, if some things had worked differently, we would have been able to stop the incinerator. [But] we had some pretty serious forces against us.

Yet they feel that they won some concessions.

Carson: One of the things we did win was that we got them to
set up an environmental monitoring program before the thing
was built. We got them to install mercury controls. We fought
for this hard, and we got [it] in.

Also, Concerned Citizens claims that it got the County Utilities Authority to use a safer form of ammonia.

Carson: Of course, they would never say we forced them to do
that, but it is clear from the history of the thing that is exactly
what happened.

Neighborhood and Community Impacts

Once Blanchard, Carson, and Parker sank their verbal teeth into their
opponents, like pitbulls, they did not want to loosen their grip. However, gradually we began to discuss their collective perceptions of what
this massive waste-management facility means for their neighborhood.
They believe that the incinerator threatens the viability of the neighborhood.

Carson: It has changed Rahway. Professor Bullard pointed out
that once you get a facility like that, it's like a symbol in the
community. People drive up and down Route 1, and people
know exactly where Rahway is by looking at that. It is on
people's minds.

Declining property values and sales were the first manifestation of
the incinerator's impact on Rahway.

Parker: Of course, we knew too that it would decrease real
estate values. That was a major concern.
Blanchard: A lot of homes are for sale. People cannot get
what they want for them either.
Carson: If I were a freeholder, I would push for, at least, a
real estate analysis of who lost what property values in the area,
and at least get that out there on the table. I'm not saying
you could compensate anybody. But at least put that information out there and say that's what happened. That's what we
said would happen. If you look at the state's efforts to site a

low-level radioactive-waste disposal facility, one of the proposals is that they would compensate people for property loss.

In July 1994, shortly after the incinerator began operating, I conducted a community survey (called a census tract) in the census area where Ann Parker lives. A total of 113 neighborhood residents responded to the survey. Fourteen percent rated their neighborhood as of "poor" quality, 37 percent rated it as of "fair" quality, 47 percent judged it to be of "good" quality, and only 3 percent rated it as of "excellent" quality. The 51 percent who rated the quality of this neighborhood as fair or poor compares to only 12 percent of the residents of New Jersey and 13 percent of residents of the United States. The incinerator and its accoutrements were the major reason for the low neighborhood-quality ratings. Multivariate statistical analysis found that the trash incinerator, motor vehicle noise, and heavy traffic and odors and smoke were the strongest correlates of neighborhood quality. Specifically, 46 percent of the respondents said that they were so distressed by the incinerator that they wanted to leave the neighborhood. Motor vehicle noise and heavy traffic and odors and smoke were the only other neighborhood characteristics that bothered more than 20 percent of the respondents, and both of these were also partly associated with the incinerator.

Two of the people interviewed in 1994 agreed to be reinterviewed in 1996. Both live within one-quarter mile of the incinerator. The interviews took place shortly before we interviewed the three representatives of Concerned Citizens. Perhaps because these two live so close to the incinerator, their views about the impacts on the neighborhood made Blanchard, Carson, and Parker's seem almost mellow. John Sabo fits the American mold of the 1990s—that is, he is self-reliant, patriotic, and believes in family. A self-employed craftsman, Sabo moved to Rahway because he could afford a house there and liked the community. He enjoys a strong family life and conducts much of his business in his home. He served in the Air Force and is proud of his son, who recently joined the Air Force. In 1994, he rated his neighborhood as of fair quality. Two years later, he rated it as of poor quality. "I would rate [this neighborhood] as of poor quality. I wouldn't want to come here anymore." Obviously distressed, Sabo spoke in angry tones.

Property values! You can't even sell. You have to give your house away. I've got contractors lined up. I'm going to fix this place up. I'm finishing my house. I'm putting it on the market. I'm getting out of here as fast as I can. From the day they broke ground, property values started to plummet. Nobody with any other choices likes the idea of living in a neighborhood with garbage trucks twenty-four hours a day. It smells in the summertime; truck traffic; who knows what we are breathing? When I call [to complain], you get the same stock answer. We're aware of the problem, we're looking into it, blah, blah, blah.

Sabo also was upset about some disorderly neighbors and the decline of some services. But his focus was clearly on the incinerator.

The incinerator is such an eyesore. And if you want to ride up and down Route 1, you can see how the highway is clean. Then, when you get in the vicinity of the incinerator, approaching it from the south side where the entrance is, you'll see all the filth and garbage that falls out of the trucks as they approach; they have trash that just blows out. If the incinerator were closed down, and the garbage was taken somewhere else, maybe out of state or to another part of Union County, maybe people might start coming back into Rahway. Nobody wants to move in here.

Mrs. Peterson has lived in her neighborhood for more than thirty years. The incinerator is about two blocks from her house and in her face every time she steps out the door.

Every time I open my door I look at that ding-dong incinerator over there. I could spit. My neighbor over there wants to go to Florida. Nobody wants to buy a house on [this] street. It [the neighborhood] was pretty nice. If you needed them [the neighbors], all you had to do was call them. My neighbor was still in Florida when the snow came. So my boys shoveled the walk so it wouldn't look like no one was home. During the summer, the same thing, he cuts her grass. Everybody reciprocates. The people are friendly.

Now Andrea Peterson wants to leave the neighborhood: "It [the incinerator] would be the sole reason. Other than that I like the neighborhood." Asked what would be the best way to improve the neighborhood, she replied:

> Shut down the incinerator! If you shut down and get rid of that . . . people would come into Rahway. The incinerator is a nail in the coffin of this neighborhood. I do think it's going to go right down, deteriorate. And maybe that's what they want it to do. Because then they can get rid of these houses, and put all industrial stuff all around this area. My theory of why they put it here is because it's predominantly a black area, and they didn't feel they would get much guff from the neighborhood.

Andrea professes no formal knowledge about science and technology. But her insights about large-scale technologies are remarkably like those of scholars who have studied accidents ranging from Three Mile Island to Challenger in the United States and from Bhopal to Chernobyl outside this country.

> Andrea: You're going to [trust] somebody who is following, and then you're going to have those that don't follow procedure and go their own way. When you're dealing with people's lives, you can't do that.

When asked about checking the data, she replied, "I know a lot of people who did that. How can I tell the reports are not fake?"

Andrea Peterson is outraged by the truck noise.

> When I moved out here, it was so quiet, I could lie in bed and hear my heart beat. I got used to the quiet, I love the quiet. When [the incinerator] came, I couldn't sit in my living room and hear the dialogue on my television. The noise from the traffic was just that loud. One time I had the TV sitting on my porch. In summer, sometimes, I would sit out there and watch television. I couldn't hear a damn thing. I couldn't open my window on the porch. When I opened my screens, the smell would come right in, and everything would get all gritty.

Despite strong repulsive feelings about the incinerator, Peterson increased her evaluation of the neighborhood's quality from "poor" in 1994 to "fair" in 1996. The reason was that the nearby bridge over the Rahway River, which funneled trucks by her home, was closed to trucks.

Now the trucks go by Sabo's home. Peterson's impression is that the bridge was not closed to placate the citizens. "They closed the bridge to trucks of more than four tons because the bridge was about to say, 'Listen, you do something, or I'm going to give up.'"

Sabo regards the bridge reclassification as a further blow because it brought more trucks to his street. "They come up and down here every day. There's no enforcement here, unless you make several complaints to the police. Then they'll send a cop by. That's about it." So the seeming contradiction of Sabo decreasing his neighborhood quality rating from "fair" to "poor" and Peterson increasing hers from "poor" to "fair" is directly associated with the traffic problem. Both strongly believe that the incinerator is the primary reason why homes in their neighborhood are not selling.

Concerned Citizens added a provocative angle to the truck traffic issue.

> Parker: One thing they could do is take the trucks away. Have a different truck route. We have suggested it.
>
> Carson: The communities in the western and northern parts of the county are supposed to take their garbage up to Route 22, over to Route 1, and down Route 1 to the incinerator. There are four or five communities in the eastern portion that are taking their garbage this way down local roads, down Lawrence Street, to the incinerator. We have suggested that they, too, go out to Route 22, and there's lots of objections, because it's a longer route. Some of the most affluent towns in New Jersey say [they] can't afford it. They could afford it, but they're not going to do it.

The growing literature about the economics of benefits paid to communities that house incinerators and landfills makes it difficult to dismiss Concerned Citizens as oversensitive to environmental equity. For example, the *Wall Street Journal* reported that what localities get depends upon their bargaining skills and power.[1] Mobile, Arizona, a poor town of about one hundred people located southwest of Phoenix, got about $25,000 in assistance for hosting a 640–acre landfill. Riverside County, an affluent area east of Los Angeles, got about $10 million a year in additional revenue for agreeing to a landfill expansion. Regarding Railway, Robert Carson stated:

The money from community benefits goes into the general budget. Originally they were going to fix up the local park and put in baseball fields. There's another field up by the western end of Rahway that is basically a soccer field. They were going to put lights in there and do all sorts of stuff. All this fell through. It hasn't happened. They've refurbished a couple of parks. They built one high-visibility playground right behind the library.

Members of Concerned Citizens argue that local officials "have used it [the so-called community benefits] politically by saying [that] the increase in local taxes has been zero, or minimal, for the last two years. But now, contract demands for increases are going to wipe out that $2.2 million 'free' money they get each year." When we asked John Sabo about local benefits, he answered, "I have no idea of how they're spending it. They're not using it on this neighborhood. They've cut a couple of trees down, that's about it."

Long-Term Battles for Local Control

On July 15, 1996, a federal court ruled that the State of New Jersey's system of telling haulers where to dump their garbage was illegal because it discriminates against out-of-state haulers. The state's waste-flow controls made sure that counties had a steady flow of revenue to pay off the construction of the incinerators. Without flow control, the incinerators would be outbid for garbage by landfills out of state. On September 20, 1996, the media reported that Standard & Poor had dropped the rating of Union County's $416 million bonds to BB, that is, to the status of speculative investments. Once again, New Jersey had a garbage crisis revolving around flow control.

Blanchard, Carson, and Parker were not surprised by the court decision.

> Carson: Why should somebody pay $80, $90, or $100 to burn their garbage when they can send it to a landfill for $30? Here they are, five years later, facing a problem that is going to sink the county, in the worst case. It could seriously damage our ability to get financing. It's just ridiculous. It's going to raise property taxes. We know that they're not going to go bankrupt.

They're going to put in some increase in property taxes. I think that what they'll do is impose a countywide, if not a statewide, incineration tax; and it will go into property taxes, or something like that, to pay off all these bonds, because they have spent, throughout the state, almost $2 billion on this thing.

Everything we've ever said about the incinerator has come to happen. We said it would be an economic disaster, and it looks like it is. They [the County Utilities Authority] are shaking in their boots.

Concerned Citizens sees the immediate solution as importing garbage.

Carson: We had predicted all along that there wasn't enough garbage in Union County to supply the incinerator. It turned out, sure enough, that Bergen County now supplies about 40 percent of the garbage to the incinerator. Now they're looking for garbage from New York. Sure, that's part of the deal. They're going to close Fresh Kills [one of the largest landfills in the world, located in New York City] and send it over the river. What will happen is what has happened all over the country with an incinerator like this: the municipality that owns the incinerator will be charged top dollar, and the people outside the municipality will be given steep discounts to make sure they get enough garbage to operate at capacity.

Disgusted and outraged by having to host the incinerator and also pay higher disposal costs, Concerned Citizens advocates an alternative.

Carson: I really think that if you did a complete analysis of the situation, financially, environmentally, and looked at the recycling markets and opportunities for composting, I bet you would come up with a plan that would allow you to shut down that incinerator, generate jobs for Union County, have a good recycling plan, and still save money over what that thing is going to cost, ultimately.

Blanchard: People [could be] taught to remanufacture and repair things that would normally be thrown out, and this job-training program could partially compensate them for teaching people to repair things.

Carson: You would sell the products that were made. So

this would be a community effort. When you're investing in an incinerator, you're putting all your money in a multinational corporation. You might as well build a pump and funnel all of this money out of your county. If you build a recycling and reuse center, you are stimulating the local economy. You're training people in employment opportunities. That's the kind of answers that we need, not dead-end approaches, with things being destroyed, and you're left with all this toxic ash.

In It for the Long Run

Concerned Citizens now has a core of ten to fifteen people. I asked them why they still fight and why they didn't leave. Kerri Blanchard looked at me as if I had insulted her. "I just would feel it's a betrayal of my principles."

Ann Parker's answer shocked me.

I have wanted to move ever since the incinerator subject came up and, of course, when it was built. My husband said, several times: "No, we stay. We've lived here forty-seven years, we stay." Now, if I were stronger than him, we would be out of here. I had been involved in other activities, such as the local NAACP, but this really got my ire.

Robert Carson's response came after considerable reasoned thought.

Carson: As you suggested, most people get into a situation like this, and the first thing they think of is to move out. That's always there. It's like a subliminal message. You want to get out of this place. But I've been in the environmental movement for a long time. I grew up with all sorts of stuff. So I had experience with social activism.

Strong family support strengthened their resolve.

Parker: My family is very much in accord with what I'm doing. My husband is in accord. My son and daughter are supportive. Some of the fellows my son works with have seen articles I've written for the paper and told my son: "Well, your mother's pretty good."

Blanchard: My husband is real supportive of what I do, and
my kids are real supportive. They are proud of me for doing it.
Carson: My kids have been proud of the whole effort.

Ironically, Blanchard, Carson, and Parker consider their very public fight, and especially their multiple arrests, as necessary to winning
the longer-term battle to maintain their community as viable. One of
the battles is to engage community support, overcome apathy, and em-
barrass those who would continue to propose massive machine technologies near their community.

Blanchard: It's hard in every town to get people involved in
things. We got the City Council three separate times to pass
resolutions to put different referendum questions on the ballot.
Three separate times, the UCUA sued Rahway to get them to
take those questions off the ballot, and they won each time
[Rahway lacked jurisdiction]. But the effort was embarrassing to
the UCUA.
Carson: The third time, I was running for freeholder, and
at the same time, we got a ballot question on there to say that
the next time there were openings on the UCUA, that
members of Concerned Citizens should be appointed. The
question won 2 to 1.

The group took some pleasure in noting that the date of the
groundbreaking had been advanced to a Sunday instead of a Monday
to avoid protest.

Blanchard: We pushed them into memorializing their unscru-
pulous behavior forever. They have these pictures of them, in
the rain, all dark and gloomy.
Carson: With their silver shovels.

Is Concerned Citizens a bunch of paranoid obstructionists fighting
phantom hazards? As I was writing this chapter, the latest of a long list
of proposals for a massive machine technology for the area was being
contested. In 1980, the State of New Jersey organized a special twelve-
member commission with broad powers to find sites for one or more
hazardous-waste landfills and incinerators. The commission, composed
of distinguished New Jersey citizens, developed siting criteria. Public

input was part of the process, and a great deal of public input was received. The criteria included distance to the nearest residence, location of underground water supplies, transportation access, and so on. All the criteria were scientifically defensible. In 1986, a consulting firm from outside the state demonstrated the implications of applying the siting criteria. They nominated eleven sites in seven counties as candidates for possible hazardous-waste sites. If nothing else, their planning exercise revealed that the application of quantitative criteria would not result in every LULU being located in an area occupied by relatively powerless people. In fact, the exercise identified some of the most affluent municipalities in the United States as possible hosts for hazardous-waste sites. It also shows what Americans instinctively know to be true, which is that affluent and politically powerful municipalities can quickly produce sufficient heat to defeat results based on objective, risk-based analyses. The original list did not include Rahway or any of its adjacent municipalities. The initial outcry from the towns, followed by multiple lawsuits and subsequent "analysis," eliminated all eleven locations.

Ten years after the formation of the commission, in 1990, two new sites were on the drawing board. The one in Carney's Point, in southern New Jersey, was on the site of a major chemical complex. This site was eventually eliminated. The second site was in Linden, on eighty acres, about three miles from Ann Parker's house. The site had formerly been used by GAF, a chemical company that produced film and other products, as a chemical plant and is heavily contaminated. Concerned Citizens, as well as other groups, oppose the site. In order for the GAF incinerator to be reached, a special exit ramp must be built on the New Jersey Turnpike. In April 1995, the Union County and Linden representatives on the siting commission were dropped from the panel. On December 24, 1996, the region received a Christmas message from the Turnpike Authority: The authority had voted five to nothing to permit the needed access ramps.[2] The language attributed to Linden Councilman Ralph Strano in the *Star-Ledger* article sounded like it had come from a Concerned Citizens notebook: "The incinerator and the access ramps don't serve the interests of the people of New Jersey. This is really based on greed and private interest." The second local source quoted in the story was Kerri Blanchard: "This is a rotten, dirty deed done to a blue-collar community. It is despicable." The GAF facility may still be defeated because a public hearing and various state permits are still required. But I would not suggest betting on the local communities.

This episode made me return to the transcript of the interviews to find Robert Carson's explanation of why Concerned Citizens still exists and needs to exist.

> Carson: It sort of snowballed. Its like a tar baby. Once you got hold of it, you can't let go.

Concerned Citizens was besieged by the feeling that the community was becoming ground zero for waste incineration. Pointing to a study done by the U.S. Environmental Protection Agency and the states of New Jersey and New York, Carson noted:

> A study of all the incinerators in the area shows that this area is ground zero for incineration: medical, sludge, hazardous waste, in Linden, Elizabeth, Rahway, Newark. One of the reasons we stay involved is that we see this question as really important and can't drop it. If you drop it, you're betraying yourself and your kids. You just can't do that, if you want to look in the mirror in the morning.

Can Concerned Citizens prevail in its struggle to keep the area from hosting every kind of objectionable land use that no one else will tolerate in their neighborhood? Frankly, probably not, and if it does, some other body will doubtless get the credit. Robert Carson articulated their strategy. "A thing that kept us together is that we don't focus narrowly. We focus broadly. We said it is 'environmental racism.' We said it's 'economic discrimination.' We said it's 'environmental discrimination.'"

My associate, George Dawson, was public information officer for the New Jersey Board of Public Utilities for twelve years. He followed the state's garbage policies. George concludes that Concerned Citizens's leadership has been remarkably successful in light of the forces opposing them. He attributes their success to a combination of tenacity; a willingness and ability to align with like-minded groups; an ability to absorb environmental, land use, and financial information; and an understanding of how to publicize their issues.

I perceive that Concerned Citizens has been extraordinarily effective in articulating its concerns. Unfortunately, the political and economic leadership of New Jersey is not listening. It has pegged Concerned Citizens as obstructionists, Rahway's Luddites standing in the way of a better life through technology in the next millennium. I have Concerned Citizens pegged as messengers who are being figuratively killed by elected and business leaders who don't want to hear the message. That message, which is being heard by increasing numbers of people across the United States, is that the power structure of the nation cannot be trusted; it uses devious and unethical practices; it focuses on immediate economic and political benefits; and it does not think about long-term impacts. In the case of Rahway, the leadership can demonstrate that some of Concerned Citizens' arguments are without merit. Data on property values and sales can be gathered, and data about local benefits can be identified. The burden is on those who are proponents of these facilities to prove that their large machines are not land-use rattlesnakes. This database can be presented to the community and updated. Committing to objective fact-finding in and by itself would increase the credibility of the leadership.

Equally desirable would be confronting the public's fear that this neighborhood and others like it across the United States are going to be bulldozed in favor of a large park for massive technology machines. If there is no plan to replace houses with factories, then someone in authority needs to say so and back up those words with a plan to maintain the viability of the neighborhoods. Part of such a plan would be to deny additional permits to what local people refer to as "poison machines." On the other hand, if the plan is to industrialize this neighborhood, the ethical practice would be to institutionalize that goal in the city plan and offer to provide incentives to those who choose to relocate, or at least tax benefits that reflect lower property values. More than anything else, the residents of this neighborhood and others like it need honest feedback and opportunities to be heard.

Chapter 6

Detroit's Arson Squad:
Taking Back
Neighborhoods from Fire

Figure 5. Jon Bozich, chief Arson Squad, City of Detroit. *Photo courtesy of the Detroit Fire Department.*

On Saturday, June 20, 1992, three Detroit teenagers decided to have fun.

> Teen 1: I was on the phone talking to my girlfriend when Teen 2 asked me to come and go outside. Teen 2 said, "Let's set a fire." At first I said I wouldn't. Then Teen 2 said, "Let's just play a trick on somebody," and I said, "Yeah." We went to the side of 111 Smith Street. Me, Teen 2, and Teen 3 grabbed a mattress. It was sitting in the backyard. We took the mattress into the house. We had lighter fluid. Teen 2 wet the mattress down. I

took the lighter fluid and wet the bed down in the back room. Teen 2 had only one match. Me and Teen 3 stood by the back door. Teen 2 lit the match and threw it on the mattress. The mattress caught on fire real fast. We couldn't light the other mattress because the first mattress caught on fire so fast. We all just ran out of the house. We watched the fire. We went across the street and stood on a porch and watched the fire. Some girls came up and were watching the fire. That's when the building fell. We got scared, and me and Teen 2 asked the fireman if the firefighters that were hurt were going to be alright. The fireman just shook his head. We got scared and ran off. I told my mother and stepfather that there was a fire on Smith Street. They asked did we do it. We didn't answer. I just walked away from them, laughing.

The collapsed building killed Roland Waters, a twenty-seven-year-old fireman who was two days away from finishing his six-month probationary period in the Detroit fire department. Waters and Steve Evans were trying to prevent the fire from spreading to an adjacent occupied house. Evans, the second firefighter was injured, but not fatally. Waters, who was married, was the thirty-fourth new member of the Detroit fire department's 1992 class. He was buried in the Firemen's Fund plot in Elmwood Cemetery in Detroit. Two of the teenagers confessed and were sentenced to eight years in prison. They could not be tried for felony homicide because the building that burned was not occupied. The death of Roland Waters led the state's legislature to change that law. Today these teens could be tried for felony homicide. The third teenager, the one who convinced the other two to play a trick, fled and is still at large.

A large photograph of fireman Waters, and smaller ones of the three arsonists pasted on a poster board were the first things I saw in the room in the firehouse where we met the three street fighters. Captain Jon Bozich had been at the fire scene. When he came into the room, he noticed me staring at the poster. After quick introductions, he said, "They killed a fireman. Arson is a coward's crime. And this guy, he talks the other two guys into setting the fire, we catch them, and then he skips bail. He's still at large. It's not ended until we catch him and he gets what he deserves."

Roland Waters's death symbolizes three themes in this chapter. First, it symbolizes the stupidity and/or vicious nature of those who set fire to kill, injure, or scare others or to destroy property. Some actions and suppositions of arsonists that you will read about in this chapter are unbelievable. But I assure you, all of the examples presented here did happen; this is not television make-believe. Second, the three street fighters profiled in this chapter, by and large, control their feelings by becoming inured to the horrors they witness. They are less able to control these feelings when a fellow officer is killed or when children are killed. You will feel their anger in this chapter. Third, and most important, Detroit, a city of a million people, has developed an aggressive anti-arson program. Years from now, I hope that arson fighters will find it difficult to recall so many examples of the kinds of death like that suffered by Roland Waters.

Jon Bozich, William Peck, and James Bush

When I did the interviews, Jon Bozich was captain of the arson investigators. He assigned investigators to potential arsons. William Peck was chief of the arson squad. Jon Bozich reports to him. Bush was administrative assistant to the executive fire commissioner. He worked for the fire commissioner. These three men have spent many hours sifting through ashes looking for clues, questioning suspects, and testifying in court. Captain Bozich spoke with us for about forty-five minutes, then Chief Peck arrived, and last, but certainly not least, Mr. Bush.

The three have shared a great deal. They were not particularly comfortable talking about themselves, preferring instead to focus on the need to fight fires. I found out that each has been fighting fires for more than thirty years, two had role models to follow, and all are infuriated by fires that kill and maim fellow officers and children. Probably the most striking commonality is that they spoke openly about the excitement and challenge of figuring out who committed the crimes, getting a confession and conviction, and working out ways to prevent fires. "Upbeat civil servant" sounds like it should be an oxymoron, but in the case of these three street fighters, it is reality. Sometimes, during the interview, I felt as though I was talking to the conductor and the first and second violinists of an orchestra.

Bozich: I got out of the Navy and had a job selling shoes in the Franklin-Simon Department store that was leading nowhere and was boring. I had a number of relatives who were police and firemen. They suggested I apply. I've been in the fire department thirty-one years and in arson twenty years. My grandfather was a Detroit police officer who started in 1913. My father was a Detroit police officer who started in 1944. My Uncle Frank was a police officer who started in 1946. My uncle John was a police officer who started in 1947. My brother Stan was a firefighter. My brother Joe was a firefighter in Detroit. My brother Vince was a firefighter in Madison Heights, Michigan. My brother Gino was a police officer in Reno, Nevada. I'm part cop, part fireman. I guess you could say I'm sort of hermaphrodite, I'm a little bit of both. This is not unusual in Detroit.

Bush: My cousin Walter was a fireman. I saw that he had plenty of time to go hunting and fishing. I also saw and heard that his work was exciting. I said that I'd love to have a job like that. When I got old enough, I applied and was accepted. I worked as a firefighter for twelve years, came to arson in 1983. Then I was appointed administrative assistant to the executive fire commissioner and have been there ever since. It's been a rewarding career, mentally and physically challenging, like Jon said. Exciting.

Peck: I didn't have anyone in my family who was a police or fireman. I was in the shoe sales business out of high school, the same as Jon was. Then I was an assistant store manager for Kinney shoes. But I had two small babies and I wanted a job with security. I had been laid off twice. I wanted a job that I knew in the future would have a pension. I admit that I was drawn to the excitement. When I got into fire service, I immediately went to the busiest company I could find. Then I applied to the rescue squad, which are like the Green Berets of the fire department. They go to all the heart attacks and car accidents; they go to cave-ins, jumpers, suicides, and all the special rescues. It was just a lot of excitement. But it started getting boring, and so I thought I'd try arson.

Many of the arsons I learned about from Bozich, Peck, and Bush were upsetting. Some of the photos in the files were so hard to stomach that I stopped looking at them. Yet, the horror that arson too frequently produces has entertainment value, like the films I've seen at least a hundred times of the bombing of Pearl Harbor. This chapter presents examples of arson that are infuriating and sickening. They are not included to shock you but to help me convey the anger, ambivalence, elation, and other emotions that these three men have felt for more than ninety man-years. They exemplify how these men have turned their feelings into a sense of duty that defies the common belief that local government officials don't feel and don't care.

Devils to Angels: Reducing Youth Arson through Public Involvement

Detroit is not the only city with a youth arson problem on Halloween. But most people associate Detroit with the problem. Detroiters acknowledge the problem. They wish everyone would also note that Detroit is the city with programs that have cut the devil out of Halloween and led city residents to call for Devil's Night to be renamed Angel's Night.

During the late 1970s, Detroit teenagers began to set fires in record numbers from October 29 through October 31. In 1979, more than 600 fires were set during the three-day Halloween period, about 400 more than the number set during a normal three-day period. The number of fires dropped to an average of around 500 during 1980–82, but then jumped again, reaching 810 in 1984.

> Bozich: 1984 was our worst Devil's Night, the worst fire scenes I've seen since the riots of 1967. We had fires burning where there were no fire companies available to respond. Houses would burn to the ground and into the basement without a drop of water. It was the worst thing I've seen on a nonriot basis.

Former Mayor Coleman Young's administration responded by appointing an Anti-Arson Steering Committee to identify high-risk areas, organize the city's resources to fight Halloween fires, and involve the community in the process. In 1986, the number of volunteers reached fifteen thousand, and the number of fires dipped to about 350. The three-day totals continued to drop below 180 as the number of volunteers reached over thirty thousand. During the years 1991–1993, this massive effort meant that the Halloween period was about the same as any other three-day period.

In 1994, believing that the Halloween fire problem was under control, the new administration reduced the focus on anti-arson programs for Devil's Night. The number of volunteers dropped to five thousand; the number of fires rose to 354. The arson squad shared a videotape with me of the 1994 Devil's Night. Mayor Archer is clearly visible in a white hat, talking to firemen and shaking his head.

Thereafter, Mayor Archer made control of Devil's Night a high priority. Chief Peck summarized what was done. First, a strict curfew was set and enforced. The curfew prohibits youth from being outside their homes without a parent or guardian from 6:00 P.M. on October 30 to 6:00 A.M. on October 31. Children under seventeen found outside and unaccompanied by a parent or legal guardian were arrested. The parent or guardian was required to come to the Juvenile Hall of Justice. A fine of up to $500 was possible, but in most cases the youths were required to do community service. Parents and legal guardians whose children were found to be in violation of the curfew ordinance could also be ticketed. Chief Judge of the Wayne County Probate Court Honorable Fred G. Burton Jr. summarized the curfew: "No longer will curfew violators and their parents or guardians receive a simple slap on their hands. They will be held immediately accountable for their actions. The swift measures we've implemented to support the Halloween curfew this year are meant to send a strong message to both adults and the children of Detroit." Chief Peck added: "The parents had to come and get the kids. The parents were irate with the kids. The media was always there with their cameras to film the parents coming to pick up their kids. So the parents were embarrassed."

Residents were encouraged to adopt a vacant house to protect, engage in a neighborhood watch program, and make themselves visible. The mayor distributed a postcard and flier in English, Spanish, and Arabic that asked people to check off if they would watch a vacant house, patrol a neighborhood in teams of two or more, call in suspicious-looking activity to the police, turn on porch lights, and either provide data entry and/or other office support or work on a phone bank. People were also asked to wear an orange ribbon to show their support for "Detroiters Standing Together Against Arson."

Bozich: Everything is blanketed. Everyone is out there on their
trucks with yellow flashing lights. We have taxi cab drivers,
meter maids, garbage collectors, volunteer law enforcement
people from the state and surrounding towns. Everybody is
patrolling the streets.

More than thirty-three thousand people participated on each of the
three days during 1995 and 1996 by patrolling streets, turning on their
porch lights, and watching abandoned buildings. Flashing yellow lights,
Devil's Night signs, and fluorescent orange baseball caps were a visible
reminder of the effort. The city reimbursed volunteers thirty cents per
mile for gas, and Ameritech, a local company, donated 150 phones and
free air time for communications.

City workers removed some of the weapons and targets of the
youths. The Detroit City Council passed an ordinance prohibiting the
dispensing of fuel into portable containers, except in emergency situations, from October 28 through October 31. Violation is a misdemeanor
and punishable by a fine of up to $500 and/or up to ninety days in jail.
On October 26, 1996, the police department towed more than one
thousand abandoned vehicles to remove them as arson targets. Between
August 1 and October 31, the city had towed six thousand abandoned
vehicles for the same purpose. The anti-arson campaign was aided by
the demolition of 863 abandoned buildings by the department of public works. Public works also collected eighty-five thousand used tires.
Halloween events were scheduled for youth at the zoo, parks, public
library, and recreation centers.

The media were asked to help, and they provided spots that emphasized that it was not cool to set fires because real people, including
relatives, friends, and neighbors could be killed, hurt, or suffer economic
loss. The media also emphasized alternative activities available for
youth. Comcast-Detroit, joined in by making twelve premium movie
channels available free of charge to all cable subscribers.

Kathryn Bryant, Comcast's general manager: This is truly a
cooperative effort to address a serious problem that has plagued
Detroit for far too long. Detroit is a wonderful city and we want
everyone to know it. By making this programming available to
all customers, we hope to encourage people to stay inside and
enjoy the evening's entertainment on cable.[1]

Chief Peck made a point of praising the media.

Everybody criticizes the media for sensationalizing. But our
experience has been that anytime we ask for cooperation we get
it. Many times, there will be a fire bombing with three or four
or five people killed, and it's a big media story. The media will
develop information that they will forward to us, and there is
certain information that they have available to them that I
don't want them to broadcast. When I ask them not to release
information, they don't. Also, when it comes to Devil's Night,
they're out there promoting ways of stopping the fires.

The police and fire department also received special training. The
arson squad saturated areas that were likely targets. Police officers received special training related to methods of responding to Devil's Night
situations, and patrols were increased in areas where a high incidence
of arson was expected.

The number of fires fell from 354 in 1994 to 158 in 1995. Pete
Waldmeir, a columnist for the *Detroit News*, wrote about what the reduction meant to the mayor and Detroit.

This was not just another political triumph, another store
opening, another bond signing. It was bigger than the Tiger
Stadium deal; bigger than even the Empowerment Zone. This
was the stuff that reputations are made of, good reputations,
solid reputations. In one seventy-two-hour period, Archer did
more for Detroit's image and his own image than all those big
deals combined. He not only scored a major victory, he kept
the city from suffering a horrible loss. Why credit Archer with
all of this? If his message had not been composed, issued, and
heard; if his people had performed like they did last year and
lost control; if luck or chance or any factor beyond anyone's
control had come into play, Archer today would be dead meat.[2]

Detroit pushed even harder in 1996. On September 24, 1996,
Mayor Archer cautioned people to be vigilant and not make the mistake he had made in 1994.

Mayor Archer: I don't want us to get lax. I don't want us to get
into a mode that I got caught in in 1994. The people of Detroit
made it clear through their anti-arson efforts that they would

no longer tolerate the senseless destruction of our neighborhoods.[3]

Newspaper columns published quotations from Detroiters on
the importance of keeping down the fires. For example, on October 3,
1996, the *Detroit News* quoted B.M., a thirty-five-year-old marketing
executive:

> Detroit is winning and will continue to reduce Devil's Night
> fires. People throughout Metro Detroit are also helping and will
> continue to work to make Detroit a world-class city.
>   C.M., a female fifty-year-old bank employee: We will and
> are doing everything to reduce Devil's Night fires. Look what
> we did last year! This is our place, our city, and if we don't save
> it, who else will? [4]

There were 142 fires during the three-day period, below the average of 195 for a typical three- day period during the year. Mayor Archer directly linked the Devil's Night success with his revitalization
goals. November 1, 1996: "Today, the people of Detroit can celebrate
another decisive victory in our fight against Halloween arson. For three
straight days, and for the second consecutive year, we worked together
to keep our neighborhoods safe and our streets quiet."[5] A *Detroit News*
editorial underscored the mayor's conclusions. "Mayor Dennis Archer
is smiling this weekend like a man who's a step closer to his dream: the
revitalization of Detroit. His latest reason for celebration is something
that didn't happen: widespread fires."[6]

Detroit's strategy is to win the fight against Devil's Night by organizing the public and then using that victory to win other street battles.
Mayor Archer articulated this strategy on November 3, 1996:

> We vowed to take the devil out of Devil's Night, and that's
> exactly what we did. This speaks volumes about any commu-
> nity that comes together. There are several things that work
> when calling for a business to make a decision to invest in the
> city, and the main question is: Does the city care about itself?
> The positive momentum we have established will encourage
> other volunteer efforts that strengthen our city.[7]

On October 23, 1996, Lisa Webb, director of Neighborhood City

Halls, articulated the same linkage in the *Detroit News:* "When you have organized neighborhoods, you have less crime and less blight. We don't just need to focus on Halloween. This needs to be an ongoing effort to support and rebuild our neighborhoods."[8] Alison Benjamin, director of Sector 5, one of the city's neighborhood redevelopment zones, added: "Devil's Night is really not a problem anymore. But the efforts unify people and do other things—particularly in areas with large numbers and motivated staff, they allow you to reach out and make community contacts. We learn which people are interested in working on which projects. The Devil's Night effort is, in a sense, really a year-round effort." Michelle Zdrodowski, senior publicist for the city: "We use the neighborhood city halls to mobilize volunteers for the city's various efforts, such as Devil's Night. These events give the citizens an opportunity to meet one another. The city keeps a database of all the volunteers, and most will volunteer for other things if you need them to." For example, the city has a spring clean-up program that parallels Devil's Night.

Reinventing Bureaucracy to Reduce Arson

Even in 1984, only 3 percent of Detroit's fires occurred during the three-day Halloween period. The twenty thousand-plus that occurred on the other 362 days of the year are handled solely by the fire department. About 70 percent of these fires are not arsons. That is, they are caused by faulty appliances, people falling asleep with cigarettes in their hands, and a myriad of other factors. I don't want to discount nonarson fires in Detroit. But I didn't pick Detroit for this case study to illustrate the need to install smoke detectors, fix faulty wiring, and take other steps that can be taken to prevent fires and stop people from being injured and killed when fires occur. Every resident and community needs to take those actions. I picked Detroit because it has the reputation as the city with the most serious arson problem in the United States.

How bad is Detroit's arson problem? No one I spoke with in Detroit or in the federal government trusts Detroit's or any other city's arson statistics. Some critics assert that the actual number of arson fires is probably five to ten times higher than reported in Detroit and other cities. Captain Bozich explained the discrepancy.

Technically, an "arson" incident is one that has been investigated by the arson squad. So thousands of arsons are not counted as arson cases. In some cities they don't have the expertise to investigate. They only find the obvious ones. In big cities, some mayors, like our previous officials, believed that reporting many arsons hurt the reputation of the city. The present mayor, Dennis Archer, believes that admitting the extent of the problem is necessary to move toward a solution.

Fatalities caused by arson are considered somewhat more trustworthy because fatalities demand investigation. Nationally, the Federal Emergency Management Agency (FEMA) reported in 1994 that arson was responsible for seven hundred deaths. A FEMA survey of ten American cities of five hundred thousand-plus people reported that an average of 30 percent of fire-related fatalities were classified as arsons. In Detroit, the figure was 46 percent.[9]

The three street fighters blame much of Detroit's high arson rate on the fact that there are many abandoned or deteriorated buildings sitting there as targets. For example, reports for the years 1994 through mid-1997 show that over 20 percent of the building fires were of vacant dwellings and commercial units. Captain Bozich discussed the link between demographic change and arson in Detroit.

> Bozich: Since I've come here, arson cases have increased dramatically. It wasn't unusual for the arson squad, back in the 1960s, to have maybe fifty arson warrants or arrests in a year. Now we can do that in a month. I think it has to do a lot with the fact that Detroit used to be a town of almost 2 million people. It was considered a residential town. Now we are down to under a million people. All those homes and vacant properties are available for fuel. Then, after the 1967 riots, it became acceptable to use fire as a protest and a way of settling disputes. Instead of trying to punch someone in the nose, it is acceptable to burn his house. The problem has escalated since I've come on the job and is now an extreme problem for the city.

In order to deal with the arson problem, the arson squad needed resources, which is where reinventing local government came into play. The mayor was upset by the increasing number of fires around Halloween in 1994. But the squad needed an accountability report before its resources could be increased. Peck and Bozich prepared a report that compared Detroit's status to those of other cities of over five hundred thousand people. The 1995 report showed that the seventeen fire, three police, and three support staff of the arson squad were responsible for 1,500 investigations and 240 arrests in 1995. This works out to 75 investigations and 11.2 arrests per year per staff officer. Detroit had the highest investigation and arrest rate of any large U.S. city. Chicago, Los Angeles, and Cleveland had similar arrest rates. New York, Houston, Baltimore, Boston, and Seattle had arrest rates that were less than one-half of Detroit's.

The arson squad asserts that it needs more resources because there are so many more fires.

> Bozich: Twenty-four [staff] is the max we've ever had, which is what we have now. That includes the chief and three captains. We were able to investigate all the arson, plus the fatal and multiple-alarm fires. Now, I reported last month that we did 42 percent of the arson reported to us. There are so many more fires reported to us. I spend half of my day trying to explain to frustrated citizens why we are not going to investigate their fire.

In addition, Captain Bozich explained that the squad's special role as part police and part fire officer demands more time.

> Bozich: We face a paradox in the arson section. The more successful we are in what we do, the less we can do. We are the only criminal investigative unit that has to conduct the entire investigation. I have to do my own reports, I have to take all the witness statements, I have to compile the warrant request, I have to take that request to the prosecutor's office to get it approved. I make the arrests, I do the interrogations, and I testify in court. If I'm doing all that going between the police and fire department, I can't be investigating other fires. In homicide and other criminal investigations, people have specialized roles. We don't. Arson is the only crime where an expert has to testify that it actually occurred. Each time we testify, we have to be qualified as an expert. That's the only crime in the country that works that way. So like today, I have nobody to assign to investigate those fires in the neighborhood near Tiger Stadium because all my investigators are testifying.

So instead of meeting you early, I was in the field doing the preliminary investigations.

For the years 1994 through mid-1997, 16 percent of the fires investigated by the arson squad were classified by investigators as accidental or undetermined. Some of the remaining 84 percent that the squad investigated were arson for fun, such as Devil's Night and the fire that killed fireman Waters. But the vast majority of the squad's time is spent investigating fires that I classified into three main categories: revenge, pyromania, and fraud.

Revenge: Gang, Family, and Other Vicious Crimes

Vicious crimes directed against people number almost 40 percent of those the arson squad investigates. But after two days of listening to the arson investigators and reading reports, I estimate that these cause 95 percent of the anger.

> Peck: Drug dealing is a business. They set examples. You don't pay and they'll go after you, or your mother or your children. Their signature is spraying the house with gunfire and fire-bombing.

The typical gang revenge against those who don't pay does not attract as much attention as gang-versus-gang arson or gang-versus-upstanding-citizen attack.

The following is a typical gang revenge fire directed at another gang.

> Gang 1 leader: On February 24, 1997, about 1:00 A.M., my house was firebombed and my mother, my brother, and my best friend were inside and were asleep. They almost died. I was at my girlfriend's house. My best friend ran outside and saw two males running. He thought they were XYZ gang members. On Tuesday morning, February 25, 1997, just after midnight, I drove over to Gang 1 second member's house after I talked to him on the phone. I picked up gang members 2, 3, 4, and 5. Gang member 3 had a forty-ounce bottle of gasoline with a rag stuffed in the top. So did gang member 4. Gang member 5 had a rifle with a long clip. I know it was a machine gun. They all got in the back seat. I drove over to P Street and dropped them

off at the alley. All of them got out. I was the only one left in the car. I saw them walk toward the house. I drove away and I know what they were going to do, burn the XYZs out, cause they burned my house. That gang almost killed my family and they are not going to get away with that. I couldn't stop my anger and had to get even with them.

The six teenage members of Gang 1 were charged assault with intent to commit murder. The case is awaiting trial. The five members of Gang 2, although known to have attempted the same crime against Gang 1, are free because of insufficient evidence.

Gangs almost always target other gangs and those who owe them money. When they go after an upstanding community member, the result is community outrage. Roosevelt Williams, a seventy-one-year-old minister, spoke out against gangs peddling drugs in his neighborhood in March 1995. A drug addict, M, was sent to Reverend Williams's home to send a message to the reverend. The addict filled a Wild Irish Rose bottle with gasoline and used a necktie as a wick. He placed it on the window ledge and set the wick on fire. It caused minor damage. Captain Bozich investigated the fire. Not satisfied, the drug dealer sent the drug addict back to Williams's home to do the job right the next day. The addict threw a Molotov cocktail through the window. Reverend Williams's wife, Eva Mae, and their six-year-old niece were killed. Reverend Williams died about a year later without regaining consciousness. This crime outraged the city. The drug addict was convicted, the dealer was tried, and the trial ended in a hung jury. The dealer will be retried.

Crimes against children and families are painful to hear about and painful for the street fighters to talk about.

> Peck: There's so much violence. I have a tendency to push it out of my mind. Sitting here and talking about it with you brings back one case after the other. We see so many burned kids. I mean deliberately burned, not accidental. Someone deliberately sets them on fire.
>
> For example, this woman and her daughter were burned. The main suspect is the father of the two-year-old. She was pregnant and lost the baby too. We believe the father took his two-year-old daughter and his exgirlfriend and doused the two-year-old with alcohol and set her on fire. This guy actually

poured the flammable liquid and set the two-year-old on fire.

A lot of times we get these fantasies when you're dealing with something like this. You'd like to take this guy behind the warehouse and shoot him in the back of the head to do society a favor. But these are fantasies. In a civilized society you can't do that.

Try to understand how angry we get. The reward is when we send these people to prison. I'll sit across the table from a person that's done some hideous act and smile at him and talk nice to him and tell him I understand. You never get anywhere with them if you start out by saying, "Okay, you piece of garbage." The interview will be over and he won't tell me anything. But as much as I would like to grab him by the throat, I'll sit there and smile and be nice to him and give him cigarettes and candy bars, get him a sandwich, a soda, so he'll tell me what happened. When he signs the confession and we go to court and get on the stand I'll look him in the eye and know that he's gone. He's going to go for the rest of his life. That's my satisfaction.

Of all the hideous arsons we talked about, the one that agitated Chief Peck and Captain Bozich most is the following.

Peck: A man was angry with his wife. They had two children, they had a nice home. She threw him out because he was violent, he was abusing alcohol, and she told him he had to go. He came back, after drinking, and knocked on the side window of the house. It was dark out. When she came to the window, both children were sleeping on the sofa beneath the window, which was their custom each night. They would let the kids fall asleep on the sofa and move them into their bedroom later. When she went to the glass and peered out, he shot her three times in the chest, side and stomach. He then broke the window out and threw a Molotov cocktail into the living room with his own two children in there. The children died there right on the couch. She ran out the back door in flames, rolled on the grass screaming. The neighbors saw this. She gets up to run for help after she puts herself out. He fires another six to eight shots at her. All the neighbors are coming out now so he takes off. But everyone saw it. They have five witnesses. She gets to a neighbor's house and collapses on the porch. They take her to the hospital. The firemen put the fire out. They take the bodies of the two children to the morgue. We recover the neck of the Molotov cocktail. We establish the crime. We interview witnesses. We know who did it.

Everyone says that he might be at her sister's house. She [the sister] says she hasn't seen him. The next day we have an informant tell us where he is. We arrest him. The wife languishes in the hospital for two months before dying. What really killed us on this was that the sister was having an affair with the husband. She lied to us. He was actually there when the police went to the sister's house. She said she hadn't seen him. This guy had just killed her nephews and shot her sister, and she lied to protect him. Our reward was getting a full confession from him and proving that he showed malice and forethought. He couldn't use the mental illness defense. He's gone to prison for the rest of his life. There's no parole, he'll never get out. He'll never see the outside.

After recalling what was a still painful memory, Chief Peck noted the difficulty of controlling revenge arsons.

Peck: We're not going to be able to develop much of a program to control revenge arson. It is rooted in psychological disturbance, alcohol, drugs, and impulsive behavior. It's like trying to stop somebody from shooting somebody else. They don't think rationally beforehand. They just take the gun or the Molotov cocktail and kill. The problem is our society's problem.

Pyromania

The Detroit Arson Squad estimates that 15 percent of arsons are committed by pyromaniacs.

Bozich: One pyro can destroy a neighborhood. When we go to arson seminars, we're often told that it would be unusual for us to meet two or more pyromaniacs in our careers. They're wrong. There's at least ten in Detroit. Most pyromaniacs will set two to five hundred fires.

One (I'll call him D) we just arrested set his first fire when he burned his mother's house when he was nine years old, and he was twenty-six when he burned his father's house down. Until we got him off the street two years ago, D had set at least four hundred fires.

He totally devastated one neighborhood. The neighbors knew who he was, but D had them convinced that he was doing it for their own good—that is, he was driving the drug dealers and evildoers out. Sometimes he set fires for them. If they needed a car burned, or needed a vacant dwelling burned down so that they could collect the insurance, he would do that for them.

Two psychiatrists interviewed D for his trial. Both want to write a book about him. When he gets out of jail, he's going to set fires. His whole life, his whole sexuality revolves around fires.

He's one of the few pyros around who always uses gasoline. The gas station attendant knew that every time he sold the pyro gasoline, fire trucks would be coming in fifteen minutes. The attendant never told anybody until we developed a case against him and arrested him. He told us: "He was a good customer. You're not going to turn in a good customer." Can you believe that guy? We were furious with him.

Every pyro we arrest has a need for an authority figure. We try to become an uncle to them, to keep tabs on them. One pyro actually volunteered to spy on D. I unofficially deputized him to do that.

At the age of thirty-three, D was caught when investigators got him to tell his story about setting fires to arson investigators who were posing as a television crew.

Bozich: We had a phony TV crew in there interviewing him. He was talking to the interviewers and confessing to all these arson fires. He took them around to show them where he set the fires, all the vacant lots. While they're interviewing him, some juveniles came up. When they found out this was a story about setting fires, they said: "We set fires, that's what we do in this neighborhood. We set fires every night." We arrested all of them.

The officers need public cooperation to control pyromaniacs.

Bozich: They want attention, they want recognition, we try to keep track of them. But they have incredibly strong impulses and will eventually give into those impulses.

We discussed the idea of a registry that would notify residents of the presence of a known pyromaniac in their neighborhood. Chief Peck liked the idea but felt that the legislature would not support such a law.

Fraud

The squad estimated that arson for financial profit was responsible for 18 percent of arson investigations in 1994. By 1996, fraud had jumped to 24 percent of investigations. The squad believes that almost every fraud case can be solved because the perpetrators are inept and scared. For example, six conspirators aged twenty-three to thirty-three set fire to a house that one of them occupied and the others had occupied. The first conspirator purchased the house for $6,000 and offered to pay a second conspirator $2,000 to burn down the house. The goal was to collect $18,000 insurance. On October 19, 1986, they set fire to the house. But the fire department put it out. On October 22, 1986, they removed their furniture from the house. The same day, one of them was observed carrying a five-gallon can of gasoline from his car into the house. A few minutes later, the house began to burn. The fire destroyed the house and severely damaged the adjacent house. The conspirators claimed that the fire was set by two "black males" whom they saw running away from the site.

Bozich: The only way we do not figure out who set that fire is if I don't have enough personnel to investigate it.

The latest trend in fraud fires is burning cars.

Bush: Right now we have a problem with car fires. People want their cars burned up either because they are clunkers or because the car is leased and they owe the company thousands of dollars in mileage fees.
    Bozich: Remember that houses in some of these neighborhoods cost $10,00–15,000, and the late-model cars cost $30,000 to 50,000.

Bush: Yes, it is cheaper to pay someone $200 to burn up the car than pay $2,000 to turn it in. The insurance company pays off the car, you're happy, the lease company is happy. The only person unhappy is the insurance agent and the neighborhood where the car is left. The arsonist reports the car as stolen, but they always screw up, they give us some information that we know from the beginning is probably untrue. We start working on that information and pretty soon we get a confession. We'll get them to give up the torch.

Peck: We arrested five or six people over one car fire. The people are desperate to avoid jail. You'd be surprised the people we get in here that have confessed to us: clergy, police, and even firemen. We also have our chop shops. They'll steal the car for what they call the front clip, the front end, and sell it to a bump shop that has to replace a front end on a car. They'll bill the insurance company for a new front end. It snowballs.

Our approach is to target car fires with legislation. The State of Massachusetts passed a law about ten years ago. If you have a car that burns, you have to talk to the local fire marshall or fire investigator and you have to fill out a form that describes the details of the fire. Under the Constitution, no one can make you do these things. But under Massachusetts law, your insurance company cannot pay you. In other words, if you don't fill out the form and talk to the fire investigator, the insurance company won't pay. I guarantee you that these amateurs don't want to talk to the authorities. It terrifies them. Consequently, in Massachusetts car fires have dropped 80 percent. We want to fine-tune the Massachusetts model. I feel confident, and Mr. Bush agrees, that this will pass because it is a bipartisan effort. It's good for everyone.

Targeting frauds through sting operations and flooding a neighborhood with investigators has become common under the new administration. For example, a Middle Eastern group moved into Detroit and opened up restaurants. While the businesses were profitable, a few of the owners decided that they could expand to larger restaurants by setting fire to their smaller restaurants. The arson squad learned that these arsons were taking place, targeted them, and made a series of arrests that ended the practice.

Most of the fraud fires cause property damage. Sometimes the stupidity of those who commit fraud proves fatal to them. The street fighters described a case: the owner of a bar that was losing money, who wanted to open up a bar in another neighborhood. The owner wanted to burn down his building to collect the insurance. With great difficulty, he convinced someone to do the job for $3,000. The arsonist poured three and a half gallons of gasoline on the floor. Before he could set it on fire, the fumes hit the pilot light, setting off a fire that killed the arsonist. He was so badly burned that the only part of him left was a foot.

The insurance industry has cooperated with the arson squad by providing funds for advanced training and by offering rewards of up to $5,000 for information.

Controlling Devil's Night has had an added benefit.

> Chief Peck: Someone else who was intending to burn down
> their house or set their car on fire to collect insurance money
> did so on Devil's Night because they figured somebody else
> would get blamed. By knocking down the juvenile fires, we
> took away many easy fraud fires. The Devil's Night program
> really works. I wish we could work it all year round.

Detroit: A Struggle Back to Prominence

The link between the need to control arson and the economic health of Detroit is striking. In 1950, Detroit was the automobile capital of the world and had a population of 1.85 million, making it the fifth largest city in the United States. Forty-five years later, Detroit has the unenviable distinction of being the first city of over 1 million people to drop below 1 million. Its estimated 1994 population was 992,000. Detroit has had the biggest population loss of any city with over 500,000 people, with the exception of St. Louis. Detroit's proportional loss of wholesale, retail, and manufacturing jobs exceeded that of the other fourteen most populous cities. For example, the U.S. Census of Manufacturers reports that Detroit had 340,000 manufacturing jobs in 1947; in 1987, it had barely 100,000.

Detroit has been in a half-century-long struggle to maintain its status as a great city. The following statistics only touch the surface of the city's pain. Among the fifteen cities that had populations of at least 500,000 in 1950, by the mid-1990s Detroit had the second highest office-building vacancy rate (Houston was higher because of overbuilding), and the highest residential property tax rate. Detroit ranked fourth in murder rate, second in robbery rate, and first in motor vehicle theft rate. It ranked first in single-parent-headed households, second in infant mortality rate, lowest in percentage of adults with a bachelor's degree or higher, highest in unemployment rate, and highest in percentage of households supported by public assistance. When Dennis Archer became mayor in 1994, he listed four missions for his administration:

1. affirm Detroit as a safe city;
2. provide essential, efficient, and user-friendly services;
3. obtain business expansion and growth; and
4. restore Detroit's financial solvency.[10]

News clips, reports, and people tell us that a great deal has been accomplished toward the second, third, and fourth objectives. An eighteen-square-mile area of Detroit was designated an empowerment zone by the Clinton administration. This means $100 million in federal grants for home improvements, educational projects, job training, and loans for about 100,000 people. Private investments have followed. In 1996, General Motors purchased the downtown Renaissance Center as its global headquarters, and it is planning to add six thousand new jobs. Also in 1996, Michigan voters approved funds for new downtown stadiums for the Detroit Tigers (baseball) and Detroit Lions (football). There are strong differences of opinion about the impact of gambling on cities, but Michigan voters approved three new casinos for Detroit. The Trump casinos, Circus Circus, the Mirage, and local interests are all vying for casino rights. Each is promising jobs, revenues, and various other enticements, such as people movers. Symbolically powerful is the fact that one of the proposals is to build a casino on the site of Motown Records, which moved to Los Angeles in 1972.

Judged by news clips, some people perceive these projects as giving away the downtown to private enterprise. The *Detroit News*, which reports these economic redevelopment events skeptically, noted that the Detroit economy is the best it has been in the last twenty-five years.[11] Unemployment dropped from 16 to 9 percent, there is more construction of market-rate housing, and property values are increasing. Three New York investment services raised Detroit's bond rating to investment grade in November 1996.

As part of its economic revitalization plans, the city government has established a Community Reinvestment Strategy, which is similar to efforts of other cities, such as Los Angeles, Richmond (Virginia), and St. Petersburg (Florida). These efforts are a textbook model of how to get the public involved. Detroit is divided into ten neighborhoods. Each has an elected board of twenty members, who are responsible for developing planning priorities for the next five to ten years. Their overall goal is to revitalize the neighborhoods using these planing priorities.

I spoke with a number of community organizers, that is, the city's representatives in each of the ten neighborhoods. For example, Alison Benjamin, community organizer for Sector 5, said:

> Detroiters are very motivated and willing to help out, but you must define the issue in a way that affects them directly [i.e., something affecting their particular neighborhood]. Detroit citizens are interested in seeing results; if they feel that a program won't bring results, then they won't get involved. They are really interested in improving areas they feel they can control or have a significant influence over. Many neighborhoods are coming back. The real estate market has certainly been on the rise; in fact, new condos selling for over $100,000 are currently being built, and the waiting list to buy these is over 100 names long. Particular neighborhoods, especially those in close proximity to the central business district and in historical areas, have been getting "regentrifying," higher-income people to move in. New housing starts are higher than ever.

In short, Detroit is making progress toward expanding business, restoring the city's economic solvency, and providing public services more effectively.

But Detroit has no hope of gaining back what it lost during the last half century without providing public safety. Crime is a sensitive issue in every big-city neighborhood, but it is the killer shark in Detroit, and arson is the jaws of the shark, the part that causes the blood to spurt. More than any other city I have visited in the United States, memories of 1967 remain in the form of derelict properties. A few parts of Detroit still look like parts of East Berlin before the wall came down.

> Captain Bozich: Arson is like a cancer in the body. If I take you to a neighborhood and have you stand on the street and then ask you to tell me how many murders were committed in this neighborhood, how many robberies, how many rapes, you can't tell me. But if I ask you to tell me how many arsons have been committed, you could point them out.
>
> People will not buy houses when they see a bunch of burned out wrecks and rubble. We have neighborhoods of mostly hard-working, lower- to middle-income families. Somebody will move a crack house into the neighborhood, or someone who makes his living by starting fires will move in. That person will burn their house or car or somebody will burn the drug dealer's house. The burned hulk will sit there for two to four years. New people won't move in. The people that live there become frustrated because they want to move but can't sell their house. So they hire someone to set their house on fire so they can collect the insurance. Now you have two burned homes. It just keeps going and going. The only people that move into the neighborhood are drug dealers, other criminals, and others who are forced to by financial circumstances. Maybe the welfare administration would move somebody into the neighborhood. The neighborhood gets worse and worse as the arson cancer spreads. Unless we control the arson, we can't rebuild the neighborhoods.

What is exciting in Detroit in 1997 is the effort to reinvent government to directly face the jaws of the killer shark. The public is being asked to participate in the control of juvenile arson, and the arson squad is being held accountable for its work. It is also being given an opportunity to be more aggressive about the way it conducts its business.

Liability to Asset: Why Not?

Detroit has taken three steps toward facing the jaws of the shark that has taken huge hunks out of it. The city has admitted the extent of its arson problem, the arson squad has been given an opportunity to run sting operations and be more aggressive about using its resources, and the city government and arson squad have taken actions to reach out to neighborhoods. In essence, the city is using its fight against arson as a test case to try to change the way government agencies work and the way government interacts with citizens. Reinvigorated city agencies, like the arson squad, and genuine citizen participation are becoming assets that Detroit can brag about.

Rather than keeping people at a distance, these arson fighters are convinced that they need more community involvement.

> Peck: There are so many good things that come out of joining with the community as far as arson is concerned. The only way we're going to dramatically reduce some of these arsons is to get the participation and support of the people whom it is going to benefit. Their work on Angel's Night demonstrates what can be done when we work together. We've got to get that spirit of neighborliness to work for us all year long. We need neighborhood anti-arson plans.
>
> Bozich: Troubled kids set fires. They become the pyromaniacs. If you can get to them before they get gratification from setting their first newspaper on fire, maybe we can nip some of it in the bud. There's all kinds of training that we can send our people to. We'd really like to get out into the community, go to the schools, and try to cut down on juvenile arson.

The three realize that they will need more resources to expand their mission into the community. They are willing to compete with other city agencies for limited resources and expect a fair hearing of their case.

> Peck: When Mayor Archer first started, he put together a Blue Ribbon committee of executives from General Motors and other companies. They went to the different city departments and conducted interviews. They picked our brains. They wanted to know what the problems were. I had a lot to say. They thanked me. In their report, they told the mayor to increase the arson squad. He did.

Bush described the competitiveness of this reinvented city government:

> Every unit in the city administration thinks their unit is the best and deserves more attention. I know we're going to have to

go through the process of convincing the mayor and his staff that these programs are a priority. What we do is gather statistics, for example, on car fires in the southwest of the city. The fire marshal puts them into a computer and we make a large map of the distribution of the fires. We try to use that information to convince the administration that we need resources to knock out that problem. Under this administration there's good chance that they'll find additional resources in the form of overtime or assistance from other agencies for these kinds of efforts. Overtime is expensive. But then it's not so expensive when you compare it to the cost of losing a neighborhood.

Peck: In the past we were not able to use our creative instincts and experiences. We're still not allowed to do everything that we would like to do, and no investigative unit in the city is going to be allowed to do everything it would like to do. There's not that much money in the pot. If the city does not have the money, it doesn't have the money. But we know we are being listened to. And Mr. Bush is our salesman.

Mr. Bush provided a final perspective.

Bush: These guys have done a heck of a job in the last couple of years. We have a growing community program from which good things have been happening. We can mobilize the community. We're really dealing with arson in an aggressive way, not sitting back anymore, waiting for neighborhoods to burn.

Chapter 7

Coping with and Preventing Disasters: The Federal Emergency Management Agency

Figure 6. Federal Emergency Management Agency (FEMA) personnel discusses recovery from floods, particularly the 1993 Midwest flood, with Michael Greenberg. Shown are (seated left to right): John A. Miller, FEMA Region VII director, Carole Coleman, human services branch chief; standing (left to right), Richard Cruse, infrastructure support specialist, Tim Burke, American Red Cross representative, Warren Pugh Jr., Response and Recovery Division director; Dennis Moffett, infrastructure support specialist. Not shown are Roger Benson and Sandy Cox, mitigation specialists, Phil Kirk, public affairs officer, and Curt Musgrave, infrastructure support branch chief.

I CAME TO KANSAS CITY to document what seemed like an improbable story, however, which is, I believe an important trend in the way the federal government conducts its business. A federal agency, the Federal Emergency Management Agency (FEMA), is changing its policies in order to reduce death, injury, illness, and environmental and property damage from floods, tornadoes, and other natural hazards. The risk-reduction part of the story is not unusual. The improbable part is that in order to reduce risk FEMA employees are being asked to end their adherence to rigid rules, be innovative, work closely with residents and local and state government officials, and in various ways demonstrate characteristics of neighborliness instead of "bureaucratiness."

Pattonsburg

I read the sign heading northeast out of Kansas City, Missouri, toward Iowa: "See Pattonsburg, the Newest Town in the USA." About thirty minutes later, accompanied by Heather, my daughter, and Jeff, my son-in-law, I crossed the Grand River and entered Pattonsburg, not New Pattonsburg. Houses with Xs drawn on them and open doors signaled that those houses were ready to be demolished. Strewn between these condemned houses were the crumbling foundations of what had been houses. I saw one boy about ten years old shooting a basketball at a rusted basketball hoop. Not everyone had moved out. The two-street-long main street, city hall, and most of the school were abandoned. As we left Pattonsburg, I saw the sign: "Pattonsburg, Home of the Pattonsburg Cap Factory, population 502." Not anymore. Pattonsburg is dead.

In 1993, Pattonsburg was inundated twice. After the first flood, residents came back psychologically shaken and fiscally staggered, but most started rebuilding. The second flood killed the town. FEMA and its State of Missouri counterpart, SEMA, offered the residents a chance to get out.

New Pattonsburg is two miles away. The new town has some of the old houses and some new houses, a main street, a school that looks like three giant igloos, and about 250 people, or about one half of the population of Pattonsburg. We parked in front of the new main street, where we met Terry and Maggie Hoover. Terry Hoover was the owner of the "Grand River Arcade and Grill," the town restaurant in Pattonsburg, and his wife owned "Maggie's Memories," a novelty shop. With government assistance they are rebuilding their businesses and community. Told with a tone of sadness, here is Terry Hoover's account of their experiences.

> Terry Hoover: This town is surrounded by rivers. Parts of it
> have been flooded thirty to forty times that we can remember.
> There were bad floods in 1947, 1973, and two in 1993. In 1993,
> the water came at us from every direction. It receded, but then

it came again. We had eight to fourteen feet of water on top of us. After the flood waters receded slightly, we rowed back into town. Spoiled food, furniture, feces from hog lots floated in front of us. Someone was electrocuted in front of us. It was dangerous.

The Hoovers and the town were devastated.

Terry Hoover: "The second flood broke the town, broke the businesses and our will."

The Hoovers praised their benefactors:

Terry Hoover: The Red Cross brought in bottled water, Anheuser Busch donated water. The Salvation Army and others donated things we needed to survive. Then the govern-ment came in. [FEMA] said that they would buy out the houses and help us relocate to higher ground. Agreeing to their proposal was incredibly painful. It was like death. Maggie was born in Pattonsburg, and I live on a farm outside of town. But FEMA told us that this was the "last train out of town" and we should be on it. We [the town] had many meetings and votes. We took a vote to support buyout and relocation. David Walford [the former mayor] was incredible. He negotiated the arrangement with the government. He worked so hard for us that he put himself out of business.

As of January 1998, 344 properties had been bought out in Pattonsburg, 82 had been demolished, and buyout had been approved for another 197. I told the Hoovers that I was here to examine the abil-ity of the federal government to help communities help themselves.

Terry Hoover: People here don't expect and don't want the government to do everything for them. They're used to doing things for themselves. FEMA came in and told us that every-one, rich and poor, in the town would be treated the same. That's the way it happened. The government brought in experts who worked with us to develop a plan for the new town. They were open to our suggestions, they didn't dictate to us like know-it-all bureaucrats. The plan the town wanted didn't materialize as we had hoped. It cost too much. Lots of people, even with government help, lost their businesses. So, it could have been better for us. We and our neighbors lost a lot. Everyone here is in debt, but we can survive if we work hard.

They [the government] gave us the appraised value of the houses. If you had flood insurance, they deducted that money from the payment, which was unfair to those that had paid the insurance. But they got us out of the water. There's a real sense of community re-forming here. I don't have much to complain about. They got us out of the water and gave us enough to try again.

The Hoovers' restaurant in New Pattonsburg, "Old Memories Cafe," has a 30–by–8–foot mural of old main street. In the mural, Tom and Maggie are holding hands in front of their businesses in Pattonsburg. There is no way the Hoovers and their neighbors could have reconstituted their town in this fashion without federal and state government help.

A lot of personal stories are waiting to be told about the floods of 1993. The 1993 flood was a slow-motion disaster involving numerous public and private organizations for periods of from two months to more than five years. The Army Corps of Engineers, HUD, the Department of Interior, the EPA, the Department of Agriculture, other national agencies, and their state progeny deserve kudos for their efforts during and after the flood. My first choice was to pick FEMA because it was in charge, and I picked the State of Missouri as the geographical focus for most of the examples because it was hardest hit.

Disasters have five stages: (1) preparing for the event (prepositioning supplies, equipment, and people), (2) suffering the disaster, (3) responding to it, (4) recovering, and (5) planning to limit the impact of another natural event. During the disaster stage, raw emotions govern many people's behavior and good Samaritans appear. I wasn't surprised to see pictures of convicts sandbagging alongside prison guards. Nor was I surprised to find other individual acts of heroism that are good for novels, movies, and television.

My second choice was not to concentrate on the late-twentieth-century cavalry riding into town to rescue people and pets from the flood. Instead, I focused on the buyout program. Buyout is probably the least exciting part of emergency management. It doesn't produce the feelings of terror associated with rescuing people who have climbed on a roof to escape destructive flood waters. I don't think Robert Redford or Sylvester Stallone will win an Academy Award playing the part of a FEMA employee offering to buy out a property that has been flooded three times during the last ten years. But buyout is exciting to those who are involved in it. Cold logic tells me that neighborhoods that are continually flooded are guaranteed to be of poor quality. The best way of improving neighborhood quality and in the long run saving dollars is locating people where they have a chance of building a sustainable neighborhood.

In a nutshell, in this chapter you will read about a federal agency moving toward decentralized management and unprecedented cooperation among different levels of government, nongovernmental organizations, and citizens. The 1993 flood was a test case for the agency and for the process of reinventing government and working with organizations and the public on a neighborhood scale.

FEMA'S Kansas City Office

In the United States, when an emergency exceeds local and state resources, the governor can ask the President for a federal disaster declaration. If issued, FEMA is responsible for coordinating the federal response. FEMA also administers the individual public assistance and mitigation programs that may provide funding for recovery efforts. FEMA was created by President Carter in 1979 when he consolidated groups working in a variety of national agencies into a new one. Its mission is to reduce "loss of life and property and protect our nation's critical infrastructure from all types of hazards, through a comprehensive, risk-based emergency management program of mitigation, preparedness, response, and recovery." The agency has more than 2,600 full-time employees and up to 4,000 temporary ones called in during emergencies, and ten regional offices.

FEMA's Region VII office in downtown Kansas City, Missouri, does not look citizen-friendly from the outside. The entrance is located on the ninth floor of a large glass office building on Grand Boulevard. I had to call the guard on the phone and announce that I had an appointment before he would open the door. These security measures make sense in light of attacks and threats against federal officials. The FEMA employees I found inside the locked doors were the most people-oriented federal employees I have ever met, with the exception of National Park rangers. I had hoped to talk to three or four people who played a key role in the 1993 flood response. I talked to nine: Roger Benson, Tim Burke, Carole Coleman, Sandra Cox, Richard Cruse, John Miller (regional director), Dennis Moffett, Curt Musgrave, and Warren M. Pugh Jr. (director, Region 7, Response and Recovery Division). The number of interviews I conducted precludes a separate description of each interviewee. Granted that it is problematic to generalize about nine people, I noted that almost all of them were born and have lived in the Midwest for most of their lives, and they have broad educational and on-the-job training. For example, their formal education includes degrees in architecture, counseling, economics, engineering, farming, journalism, geography, and public administration. Several had multiple degrees, and they clearly were challenged by continuing-education programs that helped them with their work.

The way these nine talked about their jobs was nothing like the stereotype of federal government employees. Many government employees balk when their mission is altered. It often means more work without more compensation. The following comments drawn from a conversation about the buyout program illustrate these FEMA employees' view of an altered mission.

> Sandra Cox: I was distressed by the number of children who would be terrified every time it rained. They were so scared. Now we can take that fear and other social impacts into account when we do buyouts. We can really help people all the way through. The relocation program lets us put a cost on feelings like fear.
>
> Carol Coleman: We have gained much more flexibility in the way we work with people since the 1993 flood.
>
> Roger Benson: We don't hide in our offices or behind the phone. We get out there. We deal with people. We don't tell our counterparts from other agencies what to do. We go out to the sites with them and work out any disagreements. Changes since 1993 have really helped us help people. This job is tough on people and tough on family relationships because we're so often away from home. Michael, FEMA was like the fire department. We rushed to disasters and gave funds to rebuild.

Unfortunately, we often repeated this damage-repair cycle in disaster-prone areas. Our goal now is to lessen the impact of disasters. The people in this office really appreciate the new mission. Within those communities that adopt mitigation, the cycle of repetitive loss can be brought to an end. We will never stop rivers from flooding, but sound land-use planning will curtail the devastating economic and social impacts.

The Flood of 1993 and the Response

The Upper Mississippi River Basin covers 23 percent of the contiguous United States (714,000 square miles) and includes all or parts of nine states: Illinois, Iowa, Kansas, Minnesota, Missouri, Nebraska, North Dakota, South Dakota, and Wisconsin. In 1992, a stationary weather front settled over the Southeast. Moisture from the Gulf of Mexico collided with cold Canadian air, producing months of heavy, steady rain. Cloud cover was almost continuous, and soils were wet.

The Mississippi River flooded in April 1993. When the first set of flash floods occurred, local governments responded by issuing warnings, closing roads, evacuating and rescuing people, and coordinating sandbagging and shelter operations. Local churches, the Salvation Army and the local American Red Cross provided assistance.

As the rains continued, in May 1993, Governor Mel Carnahan of Missouri called for federal disaster assistance for two Missouri counties (St. Charles and Lincoln), which lie at the confluence of the Mississippi and Missouri rivers. In July 1993, the governor declared a state of emergency in eighteen counties, and President Clinton, at the governor's request, declared a federal disaster a week later. During the next three months, the devastation in Missouri expanded to over 100 counties. Ultimately, 112 of 114 of Missouri's counties were covered by FEMA programs.[1]

FEMA and SEMA set up over thirty disaster application centers, including two mobile units, where citizens could apply for disaster assistance such as temporary housing, unemployment assistance, insurance counseling, social security assistance, legal aid, and last but certainly not least, crisis counseling. More than thirty-seven thousand Missourians applied for some form of disaster assistance.

The enormity of the flood can be summarized with numbers. A one hundred-year flood event has a 1 percent chance of being equaled or exceeded every year. The 1993 floods are estimated to occur once in every five hundred years in Missouri. Peak rainfall was recorded in most places in the region, typically two to four times average rainfall. The excess water came down the rivers in waves. It would crest, then recede and again crest. This occurred two to three times. Almost 60 percent of the levees failed to control the surging water.

In the nine upper Midwest states, 532 counties received a disaster designation. These counties collectively had a population of 25 million, or 10 percent of the national population. A total of 127 towns had to be evacuated, and seventy-four thousand people were left homeless. Annually, about $3 billion in damages occurs across the United States as a result of floods. The 1993 upper Mississippi floods are estimated to have cost $12 to $16 billion in damages.[2] The federal government spent another $4.2 billion responding. Another $1.3 billion was paid from federal flood-insurance programs, and over $600 million was loaned to individuals and businesses.

Fifty deaths were attributed to the 1993 floods. This is certainly less than the great Mississippi flood of 1927, which killed thousands.[3] But the human health cost of any flood is not known with any certainty. Mental health problems were severe in 1993 because the flood lasted eight months in some neighborhoods. It is likely that the effects of the flood went beyond the fifty directly related deaths. For example, the Centers for Disease Control investigated suicides, one of the outcomes of post-traumatic stress disorders and depression. They picked 377 counties that had suffered a natural disaster during the period 1982–1989 and compared suicide rates in these counties before and after the disaster. Suicide increased in the four years after floods by 13.8 percent. Suicide rates in the rest of the United States, compared over the same time period, did not increase.[4]

Economic costs and excess deaths can't convey the impact of the 1993 floods. The most detailed account of what people were coping with came from Peter Sturner, director of public safety for Park College in Parkville, Missouri. During the floods, he was fire commissioner for his town of about twelve hundred people located in the floodplain of the Missouri River.

Sturner: I was getting bad tips from everyone. I was angry with
the Corps of Engineers. They kept giving us the wrong predic-
tions about cresting. Some oldtimers around here told me that
the water would never get higher than the 1952 flood. It ended
up three feet higher. Fortunately, we didn't have to evacuate
residences because everyone lives up in the hills above the
river. But our commercial area was completely flooded. Water
backed up in the sewer system. We were under water for eleven
days. The sewage plant was overrun. There were feces in the
street. The mayor ordered everyone to strip all wet wallboard
and studs, remove carpeting, and so on. We had to prevent a
disease outbreak. A local chemical company donated drums of
bleach to scrub everything down.

People were amazing. A couple driving through Kansas
City stopped and helped us sandbag. They said they wanted
their children to remember this event and how people pull
together. A private ambulance company brought an ambulance
here and didn't charge us. We needed it because people were
passing out in the water from overwork. The sandbagging didn't
stop the flooding, but it saved our merchants, who had a
chance to remove their inventory. Parkville, like a lot of small
towns, has different political groups. For the first time, I saw
former enemies working together side-by-side.

Sturner was candid in evaluating a host of governmental organizations he worked with during the flood. FEMA, by far, got the most
praise.

Sturner: We got along real well with FEMA; they helped us
more than other organizations. I wasn't aware of all of FEMA's
programs at first. They came out and assessed damage to our
buildings. FEMA reimbursed us for the transportation costs of
bringing firefighters here. FEMA paid for dispatchers to help us.
They said they would pick up everything that insurance would
not cover. We had to decide whether to replace the fire station.
FEMA let us hold on to the money for a while before deciding.

They weren't allowed to fund business repair, but they provided us with the names of SBA [Small Business Administration] agencies who did.

Back in Kansas City, less than a half-hour drive away, Region VII's staff were shocked by the magnitude of the flooding.

Curt Musgrave: Three mammoth floods, it was amazing. People were under water for months. The geographical scope was huge. I'm glad I lived to see it, but I wouldn't want to see it again. When I looked at satellite imagery, it appeared like another Great Lake was forming.

He was not exaggerating. An area three times the size of New Jersey and half the size of England was under water.

Musgrave: It was trial by fire for me. I had been with the Corps of Engineers and was new to FEMA. My background was infrastructure. I was made branch chief for Human Services during the floods. The flood started slow, so I had time at the beginning. But then I had to act fast when the impacts spread across the entire upper Midwest. We were getting one thousand or more phone calls a day from the public. Many of them were being routed directly to me, at first. I had only ten people in the office to call on. We should have moved more rapidly to expand our application-processing staff. We didn't realize there would be three massive floods, one right after the other. We expanded to sixty people in the field office. We brought in another fifty to sixty people from other FEMA regions. We hired additional people for three to six weeks. At one point we must have had over one thousand reservists. Reservists are FEMA employees who are trained by us and are called to duty when there is an emergency.

Tim Burke went into the field to try to organize aid.

Burke: My job is to help people help themselves. It was tough when we started. We weren't prepared for the magnitude of this [the flood]. We hit the people with a lot of detail and paper work. They were frustrated. Then I told them that we wouldn't rebuild their levees [in some cases]. Some hated us at first. They threatened to kill me. Some thought we were going to take their land. One mayor screamed at me, "You're not taking my property."

Basically, people were grieving like [they do] after a death. They turned to their churches, and so did we. I worked on organizing the churches and other volunteer organizations. The NGOs wanted to help, but so many didn't know how to get involved. I helped form a national network of volunteer organizations. We developed a model of how the Red Cross, Salvation Army, United Way, and others could work together. Some people tried to collect from multiple organizations, so we developed a way to make sure that they couldn't. We developed a single application for the public to use.

I couldn't possibly reach all the communities. I was flying around in a helicopter because some [communities] were completely cut off. I was tired of being shouted at. It wasn't working. We had to learn how to use nontraditional forms of communication. So we made contact with the Presbyterian Church. The Christian Reformed World Relief Committee brought in people from all over the United States. We prepared a short checklist of questions for potential applicants to answer. Over thirty-five thousand people were called.

Another example is that we noticed that responses from farmers were rare. Monsanto volunteered to use its contacts in the farm community to contact farmers and alert them to benefits available to them.

Musgrave and Burke summarized lessons learned from the flooding.

Musgrave: The most important lesson we learned was to get our organization together quickly. The key step and innovation for us was bringing in reservists. We've learned to send people out in the field as soon as possible to make damage-survey reports. The ability to bring in reservists rather than hire full-time people is a huge budget savings and allows us to do our job. States are now trying to emulate our reservist program. We do more strategic planning and other intelligence exercises. We try to anticipate disasters and bring in experts to work with us on how to respond to them. The organization that goes into the field is stronger. The training, especially the personal-skills training, is better.

Burke: What we learned from the floods is going to carry

over to other disasters across the country. It already has. Now all FEMA employees are trained in working with individuals, communities, and organizations. When the 1995 floods came, the communications network was already established and waiting to go. We have an information network set to improve communications among public and private agencies. We can provide information on people's unmet needs in a way that does not require them to fill out the same form multiple times, and we have a way of providing interim funds to people. We established a network of over thirty public and private organizations. FEMA's trust level is much higher today than in 1993.

Aftermath: Prevention

The nightly scenes of horror on television and billions of dollars of damage got the U.S. Congress to pay attention. It didn't take a Ph.D. in environmental science to figure out that the unprecedented storms were not the only culprit in the 1993 disaster. Development of the floodplain was a contributing factor. For example, Missouri, which was estimated to have had 11 percent of its surface area in wetlands in 1780, had only 1.4 percent 200 years later.[5] The loss of these natural sponges meant that water moved downstream more rapidly. As wetlands were filled, levees were raised to keep water within the narrower channels. When the levees failed, the water swept away everything in its path.

FEMA was heavily criticized for being reactive rather than proactive. Critics argued that the federal government should not offer insurance to rich investors who located in flood-prone areas, knowing that the federal government would cover their losses. Criticism grew when it was learned that some properties had been flooded multiple times. An estimated 5,700 structures in the nine-state area had been damaged more than once during the period 1978–1993. Some had as many as twenty-three claims. The dollar value of the repeated claims had exceeded the value of the property several times. Distress increased when investigators found that many people waited until they were sure a flood was going to occur before obtaining flood insurance—in some cases, on the advice of their insurance agents. Critics argued that our national flood-insurance program was an oxymoron—that is, the only thing it insured was building in the floodplain. It could have been worse. A special study estimated that $19 billion in damage had been saved in 525 counties by the previous rebuilding of storage reservoirs that controlled flood waters, by levees and flood walls, and by a small relocation of high-risk properties begun in 1974.[6]

The cost of the 1993 flood forced the federal government to reread reports written decades earlier that called for proactive management of the floodplain.

> James Lee Witt, Director of FEMA, October 27, 1993: The time has come to face the fact that this nation can no longer afford the high costs of natural disasters. We can no longer afford the economic costs to the American taxpayer, nor can we afford the social costs to our communities and individuals.[7]

It was time to consider a major policy shift and a new way of interacting with the public, local and state governments, and nongovernmental organizations. The policy change removed the potential for damage by prohibiting construction in the floodplain of hospitals, nursing homes, retirement facilities, emergency and rescue facilities, prisons, drinking water supply systems, electric power generation stations, and any kind of facility with hazardous materials. It was time to consider elevating roads, bridges, and other infrastructure with a margin of safety above flood waters. And it became time to consider requiring anchoring propane tanks, gas tanks, and pesticides tanks more securely in the ground. Making structural changes to properties, including elevating electrical controls at water supply, sewage, and pump stations was suggested. Individual property owners were urged to elevate their structures; store important documents in safe places; elevate or relocate furnaces, hot water heaters, and electrical panels; buy and install sump pumps; and in many other ways mitigate against future disasters.

All of these steps make sense. I concentrate here on the buyout program, which is the most expensive and controversial policy and the one that requires the greatest sensitivity to human emotions on the part of federal employees. Governor Carnahan of Missouri applauded the buyout policy: "[Buyout represents a] departure from previous flood recovery and reconstruction efforts, which in the past have focused on the repair and rebuilding of levees and structural flood control measures. By utilizing this approach, FEMA intends to permanently remove the potential for future flood losses or injury."[8]

Federal money for the buyout program is administered by FEMA. The states develop their priorities for buyout, which are coordinated with county and municipal governments. The buyout program offers flexibility in administration, and unnecessary regulatory obstacles are suspended to speed up the buyouts. At all levels of government, the goal is to break the cycle of flooding and rebuilding.

No federal or state agency had attempted buyouts at this scale. The agencies had to establish procedures for working with each other, figure out ways of providing technical assistance, and develop expedited procedures for compliance with federal historic preservation, the National Environmental Protection Act (NEPA), and other federal rules and regulations.[9] Every part of buyout requires working with property owners, conveying to them that government can be trusted.

Richard Cruse described his role in the budding program.

> Cruse: The states identify the places and provide the list to us. We visit the locations with state people. Personally, I've looked at 3,000 to 4,000 properties. This is strictly a volunteer program. We don't take people's properties. When the flood occurs, the people say to us, "I'm getting out of here." But a year later, they say, "It's not so bad. I'll stay." We give people the assessed value of their houses. I feel for the people; they're so conflicted. They can use it [the money] to relocate or to relocate the house. In places like Pattonsburg, many chose to relocate the house because there's such a housing shortage in the area.
>
> I have excellent relationships with my counterparts in HUD, the other federal agencies, and the states. For example, we've got to be real careful about hazardous materials. When I find asbestos in a house, I am required to have someone come in and remove it. The structure cannot be demolished until the asbestos has been removed. To give you an idea, it may cost $10,000 to remove the asbestos and only $4,000 to demolish the house. We've found buried acid batteries. I call EPA and they send someone out to figure out what to do.

Cruse recounted several examples of people trying to cheat the government. Yet he feels that the buyout program has succeeded.

> Cruse: People in the Midwest appreciate what the government is doing for them. They don't have the expertise we have, and they generally respect our judgment. They're sometimes clever about demolition. One contractor removed the windows, plywood, 2–by-4s, doors, you name it, and resold it. It was a great idea. Less went to the landfill, which lowered our cost.

Dennis Moffett added:

> I worked in North Carolina doing disaster recovery. I came here to go to seminary, working with FEMA as I attended school. My job is to check potential overruns. For the most part, people have been honest with us in the buyout program. When we get problems it is because the federal regulations don't permit us to pay certain costs. For example, FEMA doesn't replace trees. When there is a disagreement, I go to the site with someone from state government and we try to work out differences. In fact, I frequently find people who are eligible for money and don't want it. I have had people turn down as much as $1,500 that they were eligible for.

When I asked Dennis why people were so reasonable, his answer sounded remarkably like Terry Hoover's.

> Moffett: It's the rural midwestern heritage. They're just not accustomed to the federal government offering to help them, and they don't expect it. People are accustomed to taking care of themselves. There is a distinct pride and preference to do things their own way. They would rather help themselves.

Linda Reed Brown, director of the Interfaith Disaster Response Network, an umbrella organization for thirteen religious groups in Missouri, focused on buyout as a way of breaking the cycle of dependency:

> Most people don't want to take charity year after year. It's a question of pride for a lot of people. Interfaith Disaster Network cannot afford to be codependent with individuals and communities who have come to rely on "free" help after a disaster. We

need to be at the forefront of the education that tells us that, in the long run, the best disaster-readiness plan is not a detailed evacuation system or a warning system that can crumble with a bridge washout or a communication failure. Rather, it is land use that eliminates the need for evacuation.[10]

The buyout program paid dividends in less than two years. The third worst flood of record occurred in Missouri in spring 1995. But the impact was much less than its 1993 counterpart because of the buyout program. More than two thousand families had been relocated out of the floodplain. As of July 1995, using mostly money from FEMA and HUD, the state had purchased almost three thousand properties out of a targeted fifty-five hundred.

> Warren M. Pugh Jr.: The limited impact of this year's disaster is a direct and unquestionable result of the acquisition of at-risk properties. While we're sensitive to the thousands of people affected by this year's disaster, we're relieved that the damage is so marginal in comparison to the 1993 flood. The thousands of people who cooperated in the buyout program successfully averted a tragic replay of 1993.[11]

From the state's perspective, Governor Carnahan noted:

> The legacy of the floods of 1993 and 1994 was property destruction and despair for citizens living in the floodplain. Out of this misery, the Missouri Buyout Program provided a financial and realistic avenue for citizens wishing to move out of the floodplain. In 1995, communities did not have to use their precious resources on evacuating residents or sandbagging private structures to save private property in the floodplain. Likewise, claims for flood insurance and applications for assistance, such as loans with the Small Business Administration or grants from the Individual and Family Grant program, were minimized.[12]

In a letter to me, Susan Stonner of SEMA pointed out that almost exactly the same communities in Missouri were flooded in 1995 as had been flooded in 1993. But only four thousand Missouri households applied for aid in 1995 compared to thirty-seven thousand in 1993. Disaster-housing check payments amounted to $4.1 million in 1995 compared to $34.4 two years earlier. SBA home loans dropped from $57.4 million to $3.4 million. She attributed the difference to the buyout program.

St. Charles County, which sits at the confluence of the Mississippi and Missouri rivers, had estimated damages of $160 million from the 1993 flood. A total of 1,374 properties were then bought out. Officials estimate that 95 percent of these would have been flooded again in 1995. In addition to the monetary savings, local residents remarked that the buyouts provided people peace of mind. They didn't need to worry every time it rained. For example, Orna Mickelis, a former resident of Cedar City, Missouri, explained, "They would have kept putting out flood insurance money, and we would have kept going back and repairing. They saved an awful lot of money. The government buyout was necessary."[13] Joe Moore, another participant in the buyout program said, "I don't have to worry about it when it rains out there. I can look out and say, 'Rain, water my grass for me.'"[14]

The Challenge to FEMA: Reduce the Risk and Expectations

The way the Kansas City Office of FEMA and its state counterparts responded to the devastating floods of 1993 demonstrates that federal and state officials can work innovatively with other organizations and citizens. To get an idea of where FEMA is heading, I read its draft strategic plan (*Strategic Plan: Partnership for a Safer Future*).[15] The document presents an impersonal snapshot of what the agency is planning to do during the next decade. FEMA wants "to change the emergency management culture from one that reactively responds to disasters to one that proactively helps communities and citizens avoid becoming disaster victims." The agency is organizing a group representing industry, insurance, mortgage lending, real estate, homebuilding, and other sectors to create disaster-resistant neighborhoods. The agency has also set forth strategic goals, which hint at its emphases. These include reducing by 10 percent the risk of loss of life and injury from hazards, and by 15 percent the risk of property loss and economic disruption. FEMA's goal is to reduce human suffering from disasters by 25 percent and to increase by 20 percent the speed by which eligible public services are restored. Another goal is to improve service efficiency by 20 percent and to achieve a 90 percent customer satisfaction rating.

Reading between the lines of this and other documents, I find three near-term goals:

1. Make the agency more responsive to disaster victims and especially to those who want to reduce their chances of being victims;
2. Reduce the public health and economic costs of disasters by putting fewer people at risk and by effectively preparing for when a disaster may hit; and
3. Encourage businesses, local governments, and the public to make decisions and take responsibility for actions that will decrease their exposure to hazards.

The two most senior FEMA staff members I interviewed, John Miller and Warren Pugh, answered my questions on these goals. John Miller, director of Region VII of FEMA, epitomizes the unpretentious people who work in his office. His family has lived on the same farm in Iowa for seven generations. He has a degree in agriculture, has been a farmer and a school teacher, has run a men's clothing store, and has worked for a congressman. I presented him the dilemma that at crisis times we know that people want simple and decisive responses from authority that will give them hope, and yet that government must not promise what it cannot deliver.

> Miller: I want us to be responsive and responsible. We need to get back to people. We need to tell them and tell them straight. We need to tell people that we can't do it by ourselves. The public needs to understand that our resources are limited.
>
> In 1994, I made a decision not to provide total assistance to some flood victims in the St. Louis area. They had been flooded in 1993 and again in 1994. After the 1993 floods, they were told that they had to buy flood insurance. We even offered to pay the first year of coverage. When they were flooded again in 1994, I would not pay to bail them out. This is the part of my job that is tough. I know most of the people are poor, that they have a hard time paying the insurance. I couldn't undermine

the entire insurance program by bailing them out again. People have got to learn to do their part. We have got to break this dependency cycle.

Warren M. Pugh Jr. was managing disasters before FEMA existed and has been in charge of responding to thirty-five disasters during the last eleven years.

Pugh: When there is an overwhelming crisis, it challenges the standard way of doing business. All the protocols, rules, and regulations are subject to change. You work in ways and with groups you had not before. Perhaps the buyout and relocation program is the best example. The floods in 1995 would have been much worse had we not gone to a buyout. Another innovation is to identify communities that have reduced the risk and match them with those that need help. Cost-sharing is another policy we are exploring. We need to give the state and local governments a financial stake in these programs. If the federal government continues to pay nearly all the money, then the incentive for state and local government to do the work cost effectively may be lost.

A big issue for us is rising expectations. FEMA is here only to supplement what states and local governments do. People expect too much from us. We don't have the budget. More disasters are occurring because we have permitted developers to earn a quick buck at the expense of all of us. They buy real estate cheap, leverage their costs fast, and when a flood or tornado hits, put the pressure on FEMA's flood-insurance program to bail them out. In 1988, our mission was expanded to include federal funds for hazard mitigation. Now we're in the terrorism business. We practiced against a nuclear detonation, and we will practice against other weapons of mass destruction.

As a society, we had better hope that FEMA's blueprint is successful and that the kind of spirited people I interviewed in Kansas City are the norm, because the United States has become more vulnerable to disasters.[16] The list of natural events leading to disasters includes hurricanes, tornadoes, storms, high water, wind-driven water, tidal waves, earthquakes, volcanic eruptions, landslides, mudslides, snowstorms, fires, and droughts.

These disasters are no longer confined to rural places like Pattons-burg. The Loma Prieta earthquake that hit San Francisco during the 1989 World Series caused $8 billion in damage. Across the bay, Oak-land was swept by wildfires in 1991 with an estimated cost of $2 bil-lion. Hurricane Andrew hit Miami in 1992 with an estimated damage of $30 billion. In 1994, the Los Angeles region lost about $20 billion when it was hit by the Northridge earthquake. As I am writing this chapter, the governor of New Jersey is flying along the New Jersey coast after declaring several coastal counties a disaster area due to a major storm, and over 3,000 miles away, urban areas of California expect to be hit with another five inches of rainfall. The Red Cross sent me a list of the most expensive disaster-relief operations from 1965 to 1996. Eight of the fourteen that cost $12 million or more have occurred dur-ing the last five years.

Unquestionably, our ability to forecast these events and evacuate people has reduced deaths. Yet it is impossible to ignore the reality that these events have become major burdens to society and a threat to our security. We have permitted people and businesses to locate vulnerable activities in places where they do not belong, on coasts where they can be hurt by storms and erosion, in arid areas where fires can quickly de-stroy expensive properties, along fault lines waiting for tremors to shake them, on dry mountainsides waiting for erosion and mudslides. Disas-ters in Florida, California, New Jersey, and elsewhere along the two coasts are much more economically painful to the United States than their counterparts in the Midwest and Plains because of the enormous difference in the value of the destroyed properties. As I write this sen-tence, doubtless someone is trying to figure out a way to convince a tax-starved local government to allow the construction of a facility in a hazardous location.

Home rule is precious in the United States, and individuals should have the right to do reasonable things with their property. Am I blam-ing the victim when I assert that if someone has rejected a fair struc-tural or relocation offer, we should not pay to repair their damaged structure, even if the victim is poor? Is it unfair to deny some kinds of new development in hazardous locations, even if the community is des-perate for new tax revenues? We need to answer these questions because a high-cost game of Russian roulette is being played with our economy.

I don't have the answers to these painful questions, but we need them sooner rather than later.

I am worried that a hazardous natural event will trigger a major disaster involving chemical, physical, or biological agents in the United States. I serve on a committee that oversees the destruction of chemical weapons in the United States. The locations I visit have multiple backup systems and early warning systems in the event of an earthquake or major hurricane. Each site has experts who constantly work on risk issues and communicate with the surrounding community. In addition, most of these chemical-weapons sites are located in relatively remote locations. When I come back to urban America, I pass by facilities that have substances that are almost as dangerous as nerve gas and mustard gas, and I know that much less attention has been paid to the implications of a hurricane, tornado, or earthquake on these facilities. The Centers for Disease Control has coined the phrase "complex emergency" to describe a disaster that affects large numbers of people through a combination of natural and human events.[17] The context for a complex emergency is assumed to be warfare, civil strife, displaced people, breakdown of transportation, and food shortages. Such a series of events is unlikely in the United States. But I cannot dismiss the possibility of an earthquake, hurricane, or tornado triggering a combined natural technical disaster in the United States.

When a disaster occurs, we respond by sending in FEMA to rescue people and aid to help the victims. Between disasters, we return to worrying about everything else. The United States is moving toward decentralized management of disasters. The resolution of disasters is going to become even more dependent on the ability of different levels of government, nongovernmental organizations, and victims or potential victims to act. We need to face the reality that disasters have become a common threat to our society. We cannot rely on FEMA to do the dirty work of reducing the risk. The states, local governments, businesses, and public must cooperate with FEMA to create fewer opportunities for victimization by disasters.

Chapter 8

Planning for
Love of Justice

Figure 7. Allan Mallach, director of Department of Housing and Economic Development, City of Trenton, New Jersey. *Photo courtesy of Alan Mallach.*

ALAN MALLACH'S office is tucked away in the southwest corner of the third floor of City Hall in Trenton, New Jersey. The interior of the office is so understated that I strained my neck, looking for a picture of Alan shaking hands with a VIP or accepting an award. Taped to the wall on an $8^1/_2$-by-11–inch piece of yellow paper was "The Mendelssohns and the Schumanns, a piano recital with commentary by Alan Mallach; music by Robert and Clara Schumann, Felix Mendelssohn, and Fanny Mendelssohn Hensel, 8:00 P.M., Saturday, February 8, 1997, at Roosevelt Borough Hall." Otherwise, what I saw was a table, a computer and printer, books of all sorts, a file cabinet—pretty ordinary stuff for the only American to be central to two of the most politically successful efforts on behalf of inner-city residents during the last twenty years.

Mallach was a key player in helping to establish the quantitative evidence and ethical foundation that housing the poor was the responsibility of more than just the inner cities, where the poor disproportionately live. Housing the poor and lower middle class, in general, and the set of cases known collectively as "Mount Laurel," specifically, are one focus of this chapter.

In 1980, the U.S. Environmental Protection Agency began a costly program to remediate abandoned hazardous-waste sites. Fifteen years later, stung by harsh criticism that it was spending billions of dollars and not producing useful results, the agency started a pilot program to decontaminate so-called "brownfields" areas and then convert them into useful community-land uses. Directed by Alan Mallach, Trenton was one of the first fifteen cities in the United States to receive an EPA grant for brownfields. In April 1997, Mallach received the EPA's 1997 Environmental Quality Award for his leadership on the brownfields issue. Trenton was selected as one of EPA's first ten brownfields demonstration programs. Brownfields, environmental justice, economic redevelopment, and their relationship to community involvement and government leadership are a second and the major focus of this chapter.

Family

Three hours after I first looked around Alan Mallach's office, I understood why it has no trophies. He doesn't want visitors staring at the walls. Mallach wants engagement; he wants us to discuss ethical principles with him, brainstorm creative ideas with him, and worry about inner-city neighborhoods with him. Mallach's family and strong religious background set the foundation for his career.

> Mallach: I'm a moralist. There's right, and there's wrong; and not always, but most of the time, you can tell which is which. It's important to be on the side of right. That's a pretty simple and straightforward philosophy. I don't think of myself as particularly liberal—socially and politically—in the conven-

tional sense. But I do believe passionately in social justice as the basic grounding of what I think my behavior should be.

Social justice is rooted in his family, especially in his father.

Mallach: I come from an intensely Jewish background. My father, in particular, was very deeply involved in issues of social justice, social service, and community service. He was very much my role model. My father was going to be a rabbi because his father had been a rabbi, and his grandfather had been a rabbi, as far back as anybody knew. But he found it didn't suit him. When I was not quite eight, my father picked up the family, and we all moved to Israel, where I spent not quite seven years of my life. At the end of the Israeli War of Independence in 1949, the Jewish population in Israel was only a little more than half a million. The country was devastated by war and had virtually no social-service infrastructure. My father spent his time inventing a social service, health service, and disabled service infrastructure.

I feel that if there is another kind of driving force, in terms of my value system, it's religion. Traditional Judaism is very prescriptive. There's right and there's wrong. There is a proper course. The word "halakha," which means the Jewish religious code in Hebrew, literally means "the way to walk." To me, at least as a metaphor, it is very apt. You set yourself a course for your life, and the kind of course you set is how you define who you are as a human being and, at least metaphorically speaking, how you are judged. You have one life and you are judged by that life.

Education and Early Work Experience

Alan Mallach went to Yale.

Mallach: Yale was a very accepting sort of place. There was very much a sense, during that time [1962–1966], that there was no one normal standard. Any reasonable way of behaving and acting, especially one that was high achieving, creative, and energetic, was acceptable. There was an enormous sense of freedom about Yale. No matter who you were, whatever your interests, there was a congenial group of people out there that wasn't too difficult to hook up with and connect with. I was lucky; they had a great program for the likes of me.

He studied music, but internships in Mississippi and New Haven guided him to civil rights issues. Alan became a land use and city planner. But his agenda is different from most planners who have become agents of commercial interests rather than advocates for residents of cities, a sustainable environment, or some other value that goes beyond greasing the money-making machine. In their book *Our Town: Race, Housing, and the Soul of Suburbia*, Krip, Dwyer, and Rosenthal call Alan Mallach "a planner-activist."[1]

Alan laughed when I called him a planner.

> Mallach: I don't really think of myself as a "planner." I found myself gravitating towards "planning" because it seemed to be the closest thing to the sorts of things I was interested in doing, which had to do with dealing with cities, housing, neighborhood revitalization, and challenging the established order. When I started getting deeper into planning, one of the things I found most exciting was the whole idea that it could be a tremendously creative field, that there were new and creative ways of doing planning, getting away from the traditional kind of zoning of subdivisions, ways of using planning techniques to preserve open space, or accommodate development along with open space in traditional communities.

Alan Mallach worked on housing issues for the administration of Governor Richard Hughes for four years. When Governor Hughes's term ended, Alan tried administration and teaching at Rutgers University, returned to work for state government, opened his own consulting firm, and then worked for county government. During this decade and a half, he began working on the issues that became the Mount Laurel land use and zoning cases.

Mount Laurel: A Landmark for Activist Planning

Mount Laurel is a middle-income community of about thirty thousand people, located in New Jersey a little over 10 miles from Philadelphia. In the early 1970s, the Southern Burlington County NAACP challenged the town's zoning ordinances for foreclosing the opportunity for affordable housing for the poor. In 1975, the Supreme Court of New Jersey held that Mount Laurel's zoning ordinances were invalid and that municipalities must permit development of housing to accommodate their fair share of low- and moderate-income housing in a region. Alan worked on these cases during the 1970s, but little happened during the next seven years.

In 1983, Mount Laurel once again was addressed in the New Jersey State Supreme Court. The court defined a set of procedures and remedies to determine each municipality's fair share. For example, the court ruled that growing communities, in particular, have the responsibility to house the poor, who will come looking for jobs, and that there should be procedures to get the desired responses from the towns. Mount Laurel II rulings led to the Fair Housing Act in 1985, which created the Council on Affordable Housing (COAH). COAH was charged with developing each municipality's fair share of affordable housing.

> Mallach: The whole thing was an utterly quixotic long shot that emerged from the thinking of a couple of lawyers in Camden who were trying to come up with a theory that would do something about an injustice that had been done to a group of black people in Mount Laurel Township. I don't think any of us had the remotest idea that it would lead where it did. One important thing at the same time—the Suburban Action Institute was making an incredibly important effort to dramatize the issue of affordable housing for the poor and get it into people's consciousness. In other words, suburban exclusionary laws were an important public-interest issue, not just something for a handful of legal or planning scholars to worry about.
>
> I worked on Mount Laurel issues throughout New Jersey and in a lot of other states. I talked to people about doing planning better not only by meeting housing needs but by regulating development in ways that were more environmentally sensitive, that preserved open space and community character. I packaged the first low- and moderate-income housing in Bedminster [New Jersey], the first project to be built as a result of Mount Laurel II, a part of the Hills planned development of 260 units. I helped set up the nonprofit corporation that was responsible to ensure the long-term

affordability of the units. I figured out pretty much from scratch how to go about doing such things, how to set up affordability control covenants, and things like that.

I became something like a professional Mount Laurel expert witness. Starting with the first Mount Laurel trial in 1972, I was part of the thinking and planning and execution of almost every important Mount Laurel-related lawsuit up through the New Jersey Supreme Court. Then, from 1983 through 1987, I was involved in the resolution of those cases mainly on behalf of the plaintiffs, both public-interest and developer plaintiffs. On a few occasions, I was appointed the master by the court. One of the things I found personally gratifying was that two of the towns with which I had negotiated on behalf of plaintiffs, after the settlement had been signed, turned around and hired me to implement the settlement.

I don't know the exact number, but ten to fifteen thousand low- and moderate-income units in inclusionary developments [were constructed] throughout the New Jersey suburbs. When I wrote my book on the subject [*Inclusionary Housing Programs: Policies and Practices*], it was incredibly controversial.[2] Now people don't bat an eyelash. It's accepted.

There's a very exciting feeling about being a part of something that is a real movement to change something major about the way the system works. Another thing is that the camaraderie, the feeling of being part of a movement with other people is something enormously valuable, and something which is rare in the world.

With hindsight, Mount Laurel seems to have been a mixed success. If you're one of those who focuses on the empty part of the cup, analysts had estimated that 145,000 housing units were needed in New Jersey for persons of modest economic means during the period 1987–1993; the Mount Laurel cases produced only about 10 percent of what was needed. Second, the vast majority of units were occupied by residents of the suburbs rather than by residents of the inner city. Third, the Mount Laurel court decisions and the state programs built to implement them have been under attack by conservative legislative elements.

If you focus on the filled part of the cup, Mount Laurel clearly identified exclusionary zoning practices as a misuse of local government power and raised the issue of regional welfare as a critical legal principle. Second, housing experts consider Mount Laurel to be a huge success because a considerable number of units were built during a period in New Jersey in which the housing market was in the worst shape since the 1930s depression. The annoying fact that few inner-city residents moved to the suburban housing is counterbalanced by the reality that moderate-income housing was badly needed in the suburbs for suburban residents.[3]

To be what one writer called the "ubiquitous figure, planner-activist" in such a morally important land-use case, and then to be on the winning side, would be a magnificent lifetime professional achievement for most. While proud of his role, Alan is ambivalent.

> Mallach: As I look back on this, somehow I feel I haven't done that much. I could have done an awful lot more if I had been a little better organized and more focused. Nevertheless, it was a success, although certainly, like almost everything else that happens in this world, a very equivocal success.

When asked to place Mount Laurel in the context of his values, the ambivalence vanished.

> Mallach: It was basically values, it came down to, This is right and this is wrong. It's funny, the principle may be simple, but the level of analysis and thinking to actually undo wrong and create right is incredibly complicated.

A Short Musical Interlude

Alan needed a break after fifteen years of emotionally draining work.

> Mallach: In 1987, I decided to give myself a sabbatical. So I spent pretty much of the next two years writing and doing music. I really started the sabbatical in the summer of 1988 and spent about half of 1989 living in Italy, doing research. I was having so much fun I had to pinch myself from time to time to remember it was real. Then I came back and started to write a book about the Italian opera composer Pietro Mascagni, who was born in Livorno in 1863 and died in Rome in 1945. He wrote sixteen operas, of which most people have heard of

Cavalleria Rusticana. I have since written and published a
number of articles about him and about other composers of the
same period, as well as record reviews and book reviews in
Opera Quarterly.

Urban Redevelopment and the Return to Trenton

Alan Mallach never expected to work in Trenton again.

> Mallach: In the summer of 1990, I was minding my own
> business, living in Roosevelt, writing the book about Mascagni,
> doing a certain amount of pro bono work with the New Jersey
> Community Loan Fund, the Affordable Housing Network, and
> helping to create some nonprofit development groups.

Douglas Palmer was elected mayor of Trenton. The day after the
election, two members of Palmer's campaign staff called Alan to see if
he would take on the job of directing Trenton's redevelopment.

> Mallach: My initial reaction was: You have got to be kidding!
> My God! I have this wonderful house. I'm living this wonderful
> life in this idyllic community. You want me to throw away this
> whole thing to get involved in what essentially amounts to a
> largely pointless struggle to revitalize a city that has been
> heading down the tubes for decades. I said, "I'll think about it."
> When my wife came home from work at the end of the day and
> I told her about this, she said something to the effect of: "I
> don't see how you would reject it out of hand unless you've
> already decided to retire." I started here in October 1990, and
> I'm still here.

Alan's statement about Trenton's circumstances is an understate-
ment. Trenton, a city of about ninety thousand, once was an industrial
center for the manufacture of steel cable, ceramics, rubber, automobiles,
electrical components, cigars, and pottery (for which it was the largest
industrial center in the United States). During its peak of industrial-
ization, over fifty thousand manufacturing jobs were in the city. If you've
traveled from New Jersey to Pennsylvania along Route 1, as you cross
the Delaware River you will see a large lighted sign on the bridge: "Trenton Makes, the World Takes." The sign is a relic of what Trenton was.

Trenton reached its peak as an industrial center almost eighty years ago. Today there are fewer than five thousand manufacturing jobs in Trenton. Indeed, when the Pennington Metals factory opened in Trenton in 1995, it was the first new manufacturing facility to be built in Trenton in over fifty years.

Alan's title is director, Department of Housing and Development. He is responsible for all planning and design, housing development, economic development, and real estate management for the city. From my office at Rutgers, when I heard that Alan had taken this job in Trenton, I figured that he had decided to play Don Quixote again. Instead of jousting with suburbs to open them to the economically disadvantaged, he was going to try to reverse the direction of the windmill and get development going in Trenton. I considered him nuts.

> Mallach: When we came to this place in 1990, the cupboard was bare. There were no programs, there was no activity. Morale was below zero. You would have had a hard time finding anybody except for [Mayor] Doug Palmer, an incorrigible optimist, who would tell you that this city had a chance of escaping Camden's fate. People told me that you've got to start with only one or two projects that you can make successes of, and only after they've happened, go on to the next. We couldn't afford that. We had to start everything at once. We had to establish that this city could move forward again, that good things could happen here. And this is true whether we were talking about housing, economic development, or neighborhood revitalization.

Housing Is Key

> Mallach: This city did not have a single line office or position that had as its mission to produce housing or to encourage housing development. The only way housing ever got developed is that some nonprofit, or some developer, decided they wanted to do something badly enough that they beat the city over the head with a two-by-four until the city did its part. We created a Division of Housing Production. We now have three

full-time people whose job is to see that every last one of the projects on their list gets built. Period. That's their job.

Alan perceives housing to be critical to redevelopment of the inner city.

> Mallach: Fate has put me in this job, so it's my duty. People have needs that can be met by the governmental system, or by the combination of government and private systems. If you're in a position to do something about it, it is your obligation to do that. It's as simple as that. If you are going to rebuild the fabric of a city and strengthen its neighborhoods, providing people with good-quality, good-looking, better housing is about the best single way you can go about doing it.

Alan's anger flared only once during the interview. It was when we discussed the current political theology of relying on the private market to build housing in environments like Trenton's.

> Mallach: It makes me angry when people talk as if producing affordable housing is going to keep market-rate housing from happening. If you have a ghost of a hope of getting market-rate housing in this city, and you spot a developer who is thinking about it, what do you think he would rather see around him: attractive, well-built, new, shiny affordable housing or festering slums and vacant, boarded-up buildings? These are the only two choices we have. If you don't accept the responsibility to rebuild [pounding the desk for emphasis] with whatever means you have, then you're saying you'll let the city fester and die. If it costs $90,000 to build a house in a given neighborhood, and the most anybody, regardless of their income, is going to pay for that house is $50,000, then you must subsidize it. You either do that or you let the place rot.
>
> Now, if I were in a city where there was an unlimited market, say for townhouses at $150,000 to $200,000, then I would build those too. I would not limit myself to affordable housing because I believe that in the long run a city that is made up of nothing but the poor is difficult to sustain. But again you have to work with reality, you have to work with the tools you've got.
>
> We take a very activist role. We talk to nonprofits,

community groups, and gather information. We figure out where the houses should go, pretty much what kind of housing it should be. We go out and assemble the sites, where necessary. I convinced City Council to approve a $6 million bond issue for site acquisition and site preparation, for neighborhood revitalization. We put packages together, we RFP [request proposals] for them.

When asked for an illustration, Alan replied:

Fairly early on, Gwendy Long, who is now the mayor's chief of staff, but was then director of Health and Human Services, and I were brainstorming and we realized that the city desperately needed a network of transitional housing facilities for homeless people. Even though there was potential funding out there, there was no player who wanted to build them. The nonprofit housing people didn't see it as their mission, and the social service agencies who could run these facilities if somebody else built them, didn't know how to build housing projects. So we created a nonprofit housing development corporation specifically for the purpose of becoming a turnkey developer of special-needs facilities. We have since completed three transitional-housing complexes: one for single women, one for single men, and one for families with children. We are currently doing design work on a second facility for families with children, a youth home for emancipated high-school-age youth, and an emergency, family short-term shelter. The organization we created also has done other things because once you have a nonprofit you find uses for it.

You look around, you walk around the neighborhoods. We have started over 800 housing units in the city since 1991. I've got 250 more that will go into the ground in the next six months. In each of the last two years, the City of Trenton has received approximately 25 percent of the entire statewide pool of balanced housing funds and low-income tax credit allocations. That's obscene.

I told him that rumor has it that Trenton has been so successful because, as the state capital, state officials don't want the city to deteriorate any further. In other words, political influence has been used to get such a ridiculously high share of these funds.

Mallach: That's bull. Until 1993 or 1994, the low-income tax
credit had to be reauthorized each year by Congress. In 1994,
Congress made the tax credits a permanent part of the Internal
Revenue Code. All of a sudden, investor interest, developer
interest skyrocketed. But they left the amount [of money] that
could be allocated constant. Recognizing that there would now
be more demand than supply, the government adopted a formal
body of rules: you file your application by April of each year;
the application has to meet a long list of criteria, and if doesn't
it will be thrown out; and that would pretty much be it for the
year. We were one of the few places in the state in 1995 that
said: "Hey, gang, they mean it." We identified all the projects
that needed tax credit allocations and were ready to move. We
made absolutely sure that every one of them went by the book,
and we did it right. We walked away with nearly 30 percent of
the statewide allocation. As far as the state goes, we get a
certain amount of rhetoric. But they don't do us any favors.

In addition to taking funding sources at their word, Alan Mallach
admits to trying to learn from mistakes.

Mallach: I've learned some things the hard way. One of the
things I'm fanatical about is that to change people's attitude,
their state of mind both within and outside the city, you must
build high-quality affordable housing. If you look at some of the
stuff that was built in this city in the 1980s, you want to throw
up. We did a project relatively early where over the objections
of some people I allowed a developer to cram an awful lot of
units onto a particular site. I decided that was a mistake. The
housing problem in Trenton is not quantity, it is quality. I'm
never going to let that happen again. We work very hard to
make sure that we are creating aesthetically and environmentally sound neighborhoods for the future, not schlock. For
example, let's say we do a house and, instead of a chain-link
fence, we do an imitation-wrought-iron fence around it. Good-
quality imitation-wrought-iron fence will add thousands to the
cost of each unit. That money has to come from somewhere,
but the great majority of people I've talked to in the community agree that it's not quantity we need but quality. Fortunately, we're not talking about one thousand units versus
twelve units or something. It's like one thousand versus nine

hundred. That's a fair trade-off. You want housing that people are going to be proud of because it is going to be around for the next hundred years.

Jobs and Redeveloping the Economy: Brownfields and Community Involvement

When we explored the issue of creating opportunities, Alan Mallach's take was different from the conventional.

> Mallach: Jobs are incredibly important. But one of the things that I've found out is that unlike some cities, we're permeable. Less than a third of the jobs in Trenton are held by city residents, and over half of the Trenton residents who are workforce members work outside the city. This means that creating jobs in the city may not be as important a goal as we tend to think.
>
> About three to four years ago, when the first round of welfare-reform hit, the city lobbied aggressively to be designated the pilot Family Development Program site for General Assistance recipients. We developed a system of taking General Assistance recipients and putting them through of process of job preparation and training. We have placed over two thousand General Assistance recipients in jobs, with about an 85 percent retention rate after a year. Most of these people were placed in jobs outside the city.

Access to suburban jobs is often cited as a barrier. Mallach had an interesting local twist on this issue as well.

> Mallach: We got a grant to study the feasibility of a reverse-commuting program not too long ago. We found that, even though reverse-commuting assistance could be beneficial for many Trenton residents, there was no employer base of need out there to support it financially. The workers managed to get there somehow. It's not that the situation is entirely good. But you don't have the measure of isolation [that] Julius Wilson points to in some of those Chicago neighborhoods, where jobs have fled. The suburbs are not an impenetrable barrier here.

Alan and I discussed land use, brownfields, environmental justice, and community involvement. Trenton has had more than its share of success stories. In 1994, a minor league baseball stadium opened in Trenton. It sits on the former site of a major industrial complex, the Roebling Steel Works, that produced steel and cable for the Golden Gate and nearly all the other suspension bridges built in the United States from 1880 to 1950. Mallach considers the stadium complex, presently occupied by the Trenton Thunder (class AA), critical to Trenton.

> Mallach: It's been tremendously valuable. It has added a level of credibility to this city as a place to visit, a place to invest in. You would be hard pressed to explain why, from a classic economic standpoint. I think you could probably measure the direct economic secondary effects in a coffee cup. But baseball still has enormous resonance. It's a good-looking facility, it has been an incredible draw [it runs 90 to 95 percent of capacity], and it has been running for three years without a serious crime problem. That's brought us an enormous amount of credibility. It's shown that there's a market here and that people will come into Trenton for sports and entertainment. It made the city and the waterfront area more attractive to prospective investors and developers. We're now talking to some very serious people about developing an entertainment complex on the Champale Brewery site [located about one-half mile away].

In addition to the baseball stadium, a developer rebuilt a former iron works into a night club.

> Mallach: They wouldn't even be wasting the gas to get to Trenton if the baseball stadium wasn't there. They are talking about a major investment. The Roebling arena [for professional hockey, basketball, family shows, ice shows, trade shows, Muppets on Ice, whatever] has gone from the category of idea, to doable deal, and hopefully within the next three to six months will become a reality. None of these would have been a reality without the baseball stadium. And we've just given a development team headed by Marriott an option on a piece of downtown property to develop a downtown hotel and conference center.

The Roebling and Champale sites clearly were "brownfields" sites, that is, buildings and parcels of underutilized or completely abandoned land contaminated by industrial activity. The tone of the conversation notably downshifted to somber when we changed to Trenton's other brownfields sites. Nationally, brownfields have attracted considerable attention from bankers, developers, environmental-justice advocates, developers, and neighborhood activists. The Government Accounting Office has estimated that there are between 130,000 and 450,000 contaminated industrial and commercial sites in the United States and that it would cost $650 billion to clean them up. In comparison, this is twice the estimated cost of remediating the U.S. Department of Energy's major nuclear-weapons sites. In other words, relatively few of the brownfields sites are going to be cleaned up in the near future. To expedite cleanup, the EPA, state agencies, and local governments like Trenton are trying to streamline the cleanup process. Local governments hope that decontaminated brownfields sites will attract businesses because sites should be relatively inexpensive, close to business-support services, and a source of inexpensive labor.

As brownfields sites go, Champale now seems like a no-brainer because of its location across the road from the baseball complex. Most sites are not like Champale. Because there is so much hype and hope about the brownfields program, I spent considerable time discussing it with Alan Mallach, knowing I would get a realistic assessment. Most of the sites do not have the fortuitous location of the Champale brewery. Typical brownfields worry Alan Mallach. They should. Trenton, by far, has the largest proportion of poor people and brownfields sites in central New Jersey. Furthermore, within Trenton, the seven census tracts with the poorest population have two thirds of the brownfields sites. Most of these sites are mixed into residential areas. In other words, there is considerable opportunity for exposure, especially for children playing at these abandoned relic sites. Residents report seeing arson, assaults, illegal dumping, and drug sales at sites. Trenton contains acres of abandoned brick, fluted-metal, and cinder block factories with broken windows, smokestacks, and weed-choked yards next to houses.

In 1991, while the phrase "brownfields" was emerging as a policy-relevant marker, I coined the term TOADS, or "Temporarily Obsolete Abandoned Derelict Sites," to describe what I see in some areas of Trenton.[4] TOADS are virulent forms of brownfields. TOADS not only need to be remediated to control exposure and to facilitate community redevelopment, but they need to be addressed because they have a history of devastating neighborhoods. In a series of interviews in major U.S. cities, I found that the worst abandoned factories, rail yards, and apartment complexes are so distressing that nearby residents seek to relocate. Areas around TOADS become abandoned. Some residents move out of the neighborhood. Many others relocate with friends and family in the neighborhood, thereby overloading those structures and causing them to be blighted. Some of these become TOADS. In other words, I am talking about a land use that becomes a neighborhood cancer that spreads and kills the entire neighborhood.

Alan Mallach and I discussed the difficulty of determining the cost of cleanup, dealing with multiple layers of government that must be satisfied, the need to get the community behind the projects, and the need to take action before a brownfields becomes a TOADS.

> Mallach: We [Trenton] were one of the first EPA brownfields grantees. We started looking at brownfields back in 1990/91, and realized very quickly that old industrial sites are significant. In 1993, when the Industrial Site Recovery Act passed and the state created the Hazardous Discharge Site Remediation Fund, we were first in line looking for funds to do preliminary assessments and site investigations. When the EPA brownfields program came down the pike in 1995, we were ready.

The details of each of Trenton's brownfields sites is beyond the scope of this book. In 1993 and 1994, the city surveyed potential brownfields sites. More than one hundred were found, including old factories, former railroad rights-of-way, parking lots, gas stations, and so on. The net result is that, as of late 1997, Trenton estimates that it has sixty-five brownfields sites on 330 acres and that thirty of these sites, covering nearly 100 acres, have been redeveloped, remediated, or are the focus of remediation investigations.[5]

I read Trenton's reports on each site, visited many of them, and focused my discussions with Alan on a few in order to illustrate his vision and reasoning.

> Mallach: My basic principle with respect to brownfields is to work backwards from your ultimate redevelopment objective, not forward from the contamination problem. The Champale

site, across the road from the baseball stadium, is the only one where we see real land value being created. If you have a site like Champale, it just cries out, "I could be a restaurant, or a night club, or a condominium, or something else." We would be fools not to use it for economic development.

The other sites are more problematic and troublesome. The twelve-acre Crane site, once a major pottery-manufacturing location, straddles the former site of the Delaware & Raritan Canal. The canal at that location has become Route 1 and Trenton's major industrial corridor. The Crane site has been remediated, and a part of it was sold to a developer who built a 10,000–square-foot facility on a portion of it.

> Mallach: The Crane site is attractive, has certain business pluses to it. I think we will be able to get serious industrial development there, but probably at the cost of a deeply discounted land sale, and possibly financial assistance for site improvement or whatever, from the city.

Much of our discussion focused on other, less-marketable sites. Mallach agrees that most brownfields sites do not have any particular market attraction. For example, the Thropp site, an old industrial facility, is partly owned by the city (through tax foreclosure), and the rest of the site is to be acquired by the city. Environmental investigations are underway. When I visited the site, I found it difficult to picture a new industrial facility on the site. Alan Mallach agreed.

> Mallach: It wants to be a public park with ballfields. You've got a school, which has no open space. You have a dense and intensely street-oriented neighborhood around it, with virtually no open space. What better opportunity to transform the quality of life in that neighborhood than to tear all that junk down and create a park and play fields?

Mallach's struggle with brownfields was most obvious with the Magic Marker site located in the city's West Ward area. The 7.5–acre abandoned factory and 22–acre site is within 50 feet of a densely populated residential area and across the street from a neighborhood elementary school. Magic Marker was the last owner, but is not suspected of contributing substantially to the contamination problem. The site is contaminated with lead attributed to a manufacturer that made commercial lead acid batteries for forty years. Environmental contamination investigations and remediation are underway.

The Magic Marker site is often cited as an exemplar of community involvement. Community residents formed the Northwest Community Investment Association (NCIA), which works on site issues and other neighborhood issues. The neighborhood group is active. For example, a company came forward with a proposal to try to remediate the lead at the site with Indian Mustard plants. The community was involved in the decision making, and community members helped with the planting. The community has its own newsletter; community members have enrolled in environmental courses and in other ways been a model of engagement.

ISLES, a Trenton-based NGO, works with local churches; helps the community with newsletters, meetings, and reviewing site plans; and in other ways facilitates the work of the local government and neighborhood residents. The efforts of this community and local government make Magic Marker among the most frequently cited examples of community involvement in brownfields in the United States. Community involvement, I believe, has brought so much attention to the Magic Marker neighborhood that the chances of site remediation in the form desired by the community have been enhanced.

But there are no guarantees that the site will be remediated and redeveloped in the image of the community. Alan Mallach is ambivalent, that is, both distressed and hopeful, about sites like Magic Marker.

> Mallach: In [its] present condition, it is a permanent, blighting, harming influence on the surrounding neighborhood. We've got to do something about the Magic Marker Site because, unless you've solved the Magic Marker site, that neighborhood will never be able to thrive. Our problem is that we've gotten to the point where we've got to start making some major expenditures with respect to Magic Marker and some of these other sites, or we will start losing momentum.

Mallach is concerned that potential investors will be scared off by liability and a perception of crime.

Mallach: I'm not sure we've got the money. One of the things that is particularly frustrating is that despite all the progress, there is nothing in the way of a self-sustaining, positive economic trend in these neighborhoods or in Trenton as a whole yet. Trenton is not out of the woods. What's happening is still very much being propped up by the energy and resources of the public sector.

Stepping back from the details of the specific sites, Trenton's brownfields program sends an important message about the need for vision. The brownfields program is part of the city's overall comprehensive-planning process for each neighborhood, not independent of the local government's overall visions of its neighborhoods. In other words, brownfields remediation is viewed as an opportunity to enhance neighborhoods rather than as an opportunity to chase out all the residents and welcome business. As the Detroit fire department has used Devil's Night to broaden community involvement, and Yvonne Carrington and Joseph Garlic have used housing redevelopment to gain community interest, Alan Mallach sees brownfields as a way of bringing the community into the larger process of neighborhood redevelopment. By focusing people's attention on brownfields and building trust through the brownfields process, the community and local government will also work together on housing, transportation, schools, and other key neighborhood issues. Mallach views brownfields as the galvanizing mechanism to attract housing, rebuild community facilities, and add public-accessible open space.

Local Government and Leaders

A local government with vision and involved communities is necessary but insufficient to improve neighborhood quality. The local government and neighborhood groups must have a competitive advantage to shake the few coins in the national and state government piggy banks and the private developer market. Trenton has slightly over 1 percent of New Jersey's population. Yet, in addition to its success in competing for brownfields funds during the period 1995–1997, Trenton received 17 percent of the State Low-Income Housing Tax Credit Allocation and 20 percent of all State Balanced Housing Program capital subsidy funds. The list of federal, state, and NGO involvements is impressive, so I asked Alan Mallach to discuss local government leadership with me. His responses are an inoculation against the common belief that government employees are bumbling fools hoping to retire with a pension and benefits before their jobs are privatized.

> Mallach: I believe that, whatever form a society may take, it has to be one which is just, provides opportunity, and shows respect for everyone. Government is an incredibly important part of making such a society possible. If government is not a strong, creative force in society, then redevelopment is essentially impossible. The marketplace just doesn't hack it.
>
> When [Newt Gingrich] talks about opportunity, he's talking about the opportunity of a pitbull to outclaw, bite, and scratch the other pitbulls. One of the most painful contradictions of the whole conservative rhetoric is the fact that, on the one hand, they idealize this romantic notion of an orderly, structured society, where everybody is happy and respects their grandparents. But on the other side, they idealize opportunity, which is the single force most capable of undermining that whole orderly, genteel, neutral society that they claim to stand for. If you look at what has undermined traditional family values, I think the unbridled marketplace has done ten times the damage of all the hippies and ACLUs and whatever, all put together. Not that they haven't contributed, but less. That whole notion of the marketplace is riddled with inherent contradictions.

Because promarketplace ideologies dominate, Alan Mallach, like me, believes that poor city neighborhoods are being triaged. Most will continue to slowly sink, others will rebound because of local leaders like Mayor Palmer, who is not about to let any opportunity pass by.

> Mallach: It *does* matter whom you're working for. If the person on top is not somebody who can provide leadership, then the whole point is quickly lost. I think that's especially true in government. Whoever is providing the leadership sets the tone and determines whether the agency or the organization will be able to accomplish anything. Life, you could say, is an iterative

process. Leaders are constantly trying things, looking at where they screwed up, and rethinking what they're doing, so they don't screw up in that way again.

Leaders have to be real. They have to accept the realities that they are dealing with, how they can work with those realities to make things better. I find it very frustrating that there are very few really good, really sharp, well-trained people in positions of responsibility in local government. Local government matters. That's where the accountability is. Nobody ever talks to the secretary of HUD about the local crack house. I wish they did. That would make our national and state officials start to realize that reality matters.

We ended on a sobering discussion of the future of American cities.

Mallach: I start to get depressed, because it is one thing to talk about Trenton, which is a manageable entity in many respects. But I look at this country, and I see a society that seems to be heedless in its pursuit of the marketplace and in its abandonment of its cities and its poor. It is very hard to feel any real hope that this country in the foreseeable future is going to take the needs of the cities and its poor seriously. No city can even remotely hope to regenerate itself through its own resources.

Mallach is keenly aware of the dangers of cities like Trenton trying to find a unique niche to fill.

Mallach: It's fun to go to Radio City Music Hall at Christmas, but that's not a meaningful part of people's lives. The people who think it is wonderful that Disney has become open to urban investment are getting it wrong. New York has become Disney-ized. It's finally come to where Disney is at. If you define life as driven by the marketplace, as distinct from community, you're not going to care about the cities unless the cities somehow generate something that's of interest to you from a marketplace standpoint. And then, you are only likely to care about the handful of our cities, and only a small part even of them, that connects with those marketplace issues, like Manhattan-world.

In Trenton, we are doing that too, because we have to work with the reality of today's economy, and our options are limited. We are consciously looking at a niche industry for Trenton, including a baseball stadium, an arena, a major quality hotel, a museum, and a performing arts center. Perhaps that becomes Trenton-world. But Trenton-world [analogous to Disney World] is important because it creates a lot of jobs. Certainly a lot of people in the four boroughs of New York City would be a lot worse off were it not for the jobs that Manhattan-world generates. This is well and good. But at the same time, it will not, by itself, bring about any fundamental transformation in the conditions of people who live in the city. I think American society has concluded that it can very nicely do without the cities. I would like to fantasize that at some point you get a kind of revulsion against the notion that our lives ought to be driven by the marketplace, and that at that point some serious thinking about concepts like community and relationships might begin to reappear. But I don't think it will happen soon.

Every city, like Trenton, I have visited can point to a new structure, such as an aquarium, performing-arts center, shopping mall, sports complex, or other trophy facility. But behind the glitz of the trophy, many—most—inner-city neighborhoods are worse off than even a decade ago. Trenton has its trophy project, the baseball stadium complex. Also, Trenton's leadership has a realistic vision of what Trenton's neighborhoods are like now and where they can be in the near future. The vision is accompanied by processes to set priorities and engage residents, businesses, nongovernmental organizations, and the federal and state government in improving neighborhood quality. Trenton's creative leadership has a moral commitment to improve every neighborhood. It is not hindered by sterile ideological dictates of how to rebuild stressed neighborhoods and help impoverished people. Because of these leaders, Trenton's neighborhoods will not be triaged as hopeless, destined for the morgue of dead neighborhoods.

A Vision of Environmental Justice and Sustainable Neighborhoods

Chapter 9

Figure 8. Charles Lee, Committee on Racial Justice, United Church of Christ, New York City. *Photo courtesy of Charles Lee.*

THE PHONE CALL from Benjamin Goldman surprised me. Ben told me that his consulting firm had been hired by the United Church of Christ (UCC) to determine if hazardous-waste landfills and incinerators were disproportionately located in nonwhite neighborhoods. Ben wanted me to help design the study and assist in interpreting the results. Although I received this call over a decade ago, I can still remember thinking how bizarre his proposal was: two New York Jews doing a study for a mostly white Christian organization based in the Midwest about

African, Latino, and Native Americans living mostly in poor inner cities and rural areas all over the United States.

I didn't know it at the time, but Ben Goldman was working for Charles Lee of UCC. On the basis of Goldman's 1986 technical report, Lee wrote *Toxic Waste and Race*.[1] The UCC released Lee's report on April 15, 1987, at the National Press Club in Washington, D.C. During that press conference, Ben Chavis Jr. coined the term "environmental racism."

Toxic Waste and Race embarrassed government officials, environmental organizations, scientists, and industries. I'm glad it did. Some of us had been hammering away at those in power not to ignore social-justice issues inherent in environmental protection. Personally, I had tried and failed to get their attention through talks and writing. *Toxic Waste and Race* did what I and others had failed to do; it had the effect of a hammer falling off a table onto a bare foot. The political outcry that followed was so loud that the federal government, businesses, and national environmental organizations have been forced to explicitly confront environmental justice. In less than two decades, environmental justice has gone from a non-issue to an ethical principle that has changed the way environmental decisions are made.

This chapter is the story of some of some key environmental-justice events. But mostly it is about Charles Lee, the director of the UCC's Environmental Justice Program. The chapter is also about grassroots activities in two places—Warren, North Carolina, and Barrio Logan, California—that Charles recommended as communities that illustrate the principles underlying environmental justice and sustainable communities. Charles and I discussed two other places. Both of them—Chester (chapter 1) and Trenton (chapter 8)—are in this book.

The United Church of Christ's Environmental Justice Program and Charles Lee

The United Church of Christ, constituted in 1957, is headquartered in Cleveland, Ohio, and has over six thousand churches in the United States. The UCC combined two much older Protestant denominations, the Evangelical and Reformed and the Congregational. With about 1.6 million members, the UCC is about the same size as the Episcopal

Church and smaller than the Presbyterian Church (2.7 million members), Evangelical Lutheran Church of America (3.9 million), and Southern Baptist Convention (15.4 million).

> Lee: The United Church of Christ is a small, mainline Protestant denomination. Ninety-four percent of the members are white. The church is socially active. Social activism goes back to the part of the church called the American Missionary Association, which played a role in the abolitionist movement. You'll probably see the movie about the Armistad rebellion, where slaves rebelled on a ship and made the case that they weren't slaves. They were found to be free people and went back to Africa. This incident is part of the United Church of Christ's history. One way of putting it is that this church is a lot more flexible, caring, and down-to-earth than most.
>
> The link to social activism is through the Congregationalists, whose roots in New England date back to the Puritans. They were among the first to champion education for women [Mt. Holyoke and Oberlin] and to have missionary organizations that reached both the American frontier and overseas. Beyond their involvement in the Armistad rebellion, by 1838, their American Missionary association was the ranking organization in the United States for the betterment of freed slaves.
>
> The Commission for Racial Justice is the civil rights agency of the UCC. In the 1960s, every denomination had an entity devoted to civil rights and racial justice. Over the next several decades, as issues of civil rights and racial justice went out of vogue, the other denominations either abolished or subsumed these units. The UCC became the only Protestant denomination to have a free-standing, full-time agency focused around civil rights and racial justice. The existence of this agency has allowed us to address issues like environmental racism. In the early 1980s, the commission had offices in New York, Washington, and North Carolina.

Charles described how the UCC became involved in the environmental-justice movement.

> Lee: There was an issue in Warren County, North Carolina. Warren was one of the poorest counties in the state and I think

had the highest or one of the highest percentages of black people in North Carolina. The state picked it as the place to put soil contaminated with illegally dumped PCBs. The waste had been illegally dumped in fourteen counties over 210 miles of highways. Throughout the state of North Carolina, they chose this county for the PCB landfill.

PCBs were widely used as insulating materials, lubricants, and coolants in transformers and other electrical equipment. PCB manufacture in the United States stopped in 1977 because of evidence of health effects in animals, including kidney, liver, and skin damage. Some forms of PCBs seemed to increase cancer risk in animals. PCBs' effects on humans are unclear. Nevertheless, the weight of animal evidence is so strong that PCBs rank sixth on the Agency for Toxic Substances and Disease Registry list of hazards, and PCBs are included in the EPA's list of top twenty hazardous substances.

> Lee: Residents of Warren County came to the commission for assistance [about the PCB landfill]. The person responsible for the commission's office in North Carolina was Reverend Leon White. Leon was involved in the civil rights struggle in North Carolina and other places for decades, and he was a church pastor. Leon had the experience and knew what to do. He made a call for civil rights organizations to become involved. The Southern Christian Leadership Conference got involved. Reverend White catalyzed a series of events that led to the arrest of over five hundred people who put their bodies in front of trucks that carried the PCB-laden soil into the site. It was an interesting mix of people and groups that transformed a local environmental struggle into a national movement for environmental justice.
>
> Warren County wasn't a unique event. It was no different than a lot of other waste-management and toxic exposure situations in the country. I know you know that the largest hazardous-waste landfill is located in a predominantly black community in Alabama, that black and Latino children are disproportionately suffering from lead poisoning and childhood asthma, and that poisoned pesticide workers are disproportionately Latino. Blacks live proximate to noxious industries in every region in the country from Louisiana's cancer alley to

California's Richmond to Chicago's South Side, and, of course, Chester [Pennsylvania]. Native Americans end up with lung cancer after working in uranium ore mining, and their communities are locations for nuclear- and hazardous-waste facilities. The "maquiladora" communities on the U.S.-Mexico border have few environmental or occupational codes, terrible sanitation and public health services. Out of all of these and more, Warren County got national media recognition. It was a real spark. It was then that the commission embarked on the study of environmental justice. Charles Cobb, the director, and Ben Chavis, the deputy director of the commission, were the major leaders, along, of course, with Reverend White.

Charles described his background and his involvement in the UCC program.

Lee: I was born in Taiwan. I came to this country when I was eight, so I grew up here. I'm part of the one-and-a-half generation—that is, not born here but schooled here and acculturated here. My dad was a chemist. He came here to study and work. He was really interested in our being successful, the striving of the immigrant. He was intense. He wanted us to go to good colleges.

I ended up going to Harvard for two years but not finishing there. It was the end of the 1960s. The country was traumatized. Young people like me were searching for identity. All the foment with civil rights with African Americans had a profound impact on Asian American identity, searching for, trying to understand who they were. One of the books that had a big influence on me was Malcolm X's autobiography. When I was at Harvard, I would talk to people about Malcolm X.

I decided to leave school and get involved with groups emerging around the issue of civil rights. I went to work for the hospital workers union [District 1199]. Then I went to work for the New Jersey Committee for Occupational Safety and Health. I was working on health and safety issues, mostly among blacks and Latino workers, when the incident in Warren County happened. Under the New Jersey Committee for Occupational Health and Safety, we organized a group of people to go down to Warren County. I thought this was a very important happening. I had written my first article about race, poverty, and the environment in the mid-1970s, so I could see the importance of Warren County.

The people [in Warren County] were being very logical. They wanted to know why the PCBs couldn't be shipped to Alabama. [The largest hazardous-waste landfill in the United States, the so-called "Cadillac of dumps," is in rural Emelle, Alabama.] This was 1982. I thought there was a real story here, so I organized a tour. Reverend White; Ken Ferruccio, a former English professor who ended up relocating to North Carolina near the site; and Dollie Burwell, an activist and member of the UCC came. When I got to New York, I wanted the UCC to be involved. I met Ben Chavis and Dr. Cobb. That's how my association with the UCC started.

Charles described how he got the idea for the work that led to *Toxic Waste and Race*.

Lee: I needed to put this issue on the map in a way that would galvanize our understanding, to make the issue perceivable. I was telling my wife that once in a lifetime you may come up with one or two truly original ideas. That was the truly original idea. One of the things that has been gratifying is that people, attorneys, have come to me and said: "I saw that report, and that helped me to make my career choice."

Also gratifying to Charles Lee has been the support of his family.

Lee: My wife has always been on my case to explain to my two children [Christopher, an accountant who lives in San Francisco, and Jessica, a student at Stuyvesant High School in New York City] what I do. I've always had a hard time. My daughter, Jessica, edited a chapter I wrote, "Environmental Justice: Creating a Vision for Achieving Health and Sustainable Communities." One day after reading this, she came up to me, gave me a big hug, and said, "You know, I really like what you do."

Warren County, Then and Now

Before we left the discussion of the birth of the environmental-justice movement, Charles, who prefers to divert attention away from himself, suggested that I follow-up and see what has transpired in Warren County. So I did. In 1982, Warren County, North Carolina, had a population of 16,200 people. The population was 60 percent black, which was the second-highest proportion in a state with one hundred counties. Warren also had the second-highest proportion of families with incomes below the poverty level and the second-lowest percentage of persons who had graduated high school. Warren was an economically stressed place in 1982, even before the PCB landfill.

The demographics of Warren County have not changed much since 1982. The population grew from 16,200 in 1982 to almost 18,000 in 1995. In 1990, the proportion of black residents was 57 percent, third highest in the state. The proportion of high school graduates increased from second lowest of one hundred counties in 1980 to third lowest in 1990. The proportion of families below the poverty level stood at almost 25 percent in 1989, the highest in North Carolina. Warren County was a poor place in 1982, it is poor in 1998, and it is difficult to see how its residents will become less impoverished.

The landfill has not helped. Massenberg Kearney lives about one-half mile from the site.

> Kearney: Sometimes it seems like we're in the same place we were in 1982. There's nothing I can really put my hands on. When I have health problems or when a lot of my animals die, I do wonder if it has anything to do with the landfill. Is the landfill leaking? Is the health of my family in danger? What is the state doing to clean up the site? And why did the state choose my community to contain hazardous waste?[2]

The answer to the Why question was provided by Bill Meyer, director of the Division of Waste Management for North Carolina's Department of Environment, Health, and Natural Resources.

> Meyer: We looked at ninety-three sites in thirteen counties and considered several factors in making a decision, such as soil characteristics of the area and the population density—the site that would affect the least amount of people.[3]

The PCB landfill site near the small town of Afton (sixteen hundred people, 85 percent African American) eventually received more than six thousand truckloads of contaminated soil. Dollie Burwell, who was part of Charles Lee's tour of the area in 1982, has strong views of what happened in the community.

> Burwell: It's a gross injustice any time a toxic waste facility is put in a community that is already destitute. Not only do we wonder about our health, but the landfill has had a negative impact on the value of our land.

She added that many children at the local school would not drink the water.

Sixteen years after North Carolina constructed the landfill in Warren County, the landfill remains a big issue. There is no direct evidence that the landfill is exposing people to toxins, but local concern exists. According to USEPA documents, there is ten to fifteen feet of standing water in the landfill. The liner on top of the landfill is compromised, which means that a rupture could discharge toxins into the ground and air. EPA is requiring the state to upgrade the ability of equipment to remove the contaminated material from the landfill. Joel Hirschhorn, a well-known environmental-policy expert at the national level, is acting as science advisor to the Joint Warren County/State PCB Landfill Working Group. Hirschhorn believes the landfill is leaking, and he is concerned about air and soil emissions.

> Hirschhorn: We have hard evidence that there are cracks in the top liner of the landfill, which is why it's not surprising that we've found PCB air emissions.[4]

Hirschhorn has called for detoxifying the wastes in the landfill.

> Hirschhorn: Detoxifying is an expensive proposition. But it's worth it to the people who live there.
>
> Meyer: We plan to make the repairs, and we are also working on selecting a feasible technology to detoxify the landfill. We are getting cost estimates and expect it will cost $20 to $30 million to detoxify the landfill. Then we'll go to the General Assembly to request the funds. The state legislature, of course, may or may not appropriate the funds.[5]

As a result of these disclosures, some residents have decided to move, and some others have installed water filters. Others will stick it out. Says Massenberg Kearney, one of those who has installed water filters, "I was born here and own 35 acres of land in this area. I can't just pick up and leave. This is my home."[6]

Warren County, in Charles Lee's words, is the "place that transformed a local environmental struggle into a national movement for environmental justice and now sustainable communities." Warren's historical status has not translated to better neighborhood quality.

Sustainable Communities

I told Charles Lee that middle-class Americans use the expression "sustainable development" as justification for erecting land use and environmental walls around their neighborhoods, which guarantees that every LULU ends up in an inner-city or poor rural neighborhood. Charles didn't disagree. Part of the environmental-justice outcry in the United States has been aimed at the large, national environmental organizations that have focused on preserving wildlife, endangered species, and open spaces. In the early 1970s, the membership of the Sierra Club, in fact, went on record as opposed to increasing involvement with urban poor and minorities by a three-to-one vote.

Yet Lee argues that the concept of sustainable communities is more relevant to inner cities than to affluent suburbs because of the greater need for a neighborhood vision.

> Lee: We need to look at communities holistically. We need to train technical people to look beyond their compartmentalized approaches toward a more holistic view of communities. Let's use the Institute of Medicine [IOM] report to help define "sustainable community." The IOM said that two conditions were necessary to assure a healthy public. One was scientific and technical knowledge. The second was organized community efforts aimed at preventing disease and promoting health. The World Health Organization defines health as physical, mental, and social well-being, and it defines a healthy community as one that is clean, safe, provides basic needs, including health care, and a vital economy. Both of those definitions, which I have paraphrased, are consistent with what I see as the paradigm of sustainable communities. It is based on bottom-up,

holistic, community-based, multi-issue, integrative, interdependent, and unifying views of neighborhood and community. As an activist agency, our philosophy is that grassroots leadership development, community empowerment, and the development of local capacity are key to long-term solutions.

Lee views the grassroots movement as attempting to control what is going on in its environment and to build a critical mass to change society's way of managing resources. He contrasts this view of environment with what he considers reductionist thinking by the national and state government and business, which have legitimized geographically concentrated human exposure to harmful substances, crime, and blight on "other side of the track" neighborhoods.

Lee: Environmental justice came from all those communities that began to raise issues and make connections for themselves. When I talk about a new paradigm of development, it has to be place-based and community-based. It has to reorient and direct our understanding and application of science to value-based understanding of society, community, family, morals, and ethics.

My job is to discern the signs of hope. An enduring and abiding goal of environmental justice is a constant search for truly authentic signs of hope. I see them in many places. There are local groups working on transportation, on the environment, on environmental education, on pollution prevention, on agriculture, on greening of urban places, on Native American reservations. They see the direct link to environmental justice. There are groups working on international trade, and they see the link with environmental justice; workers working on health and safety issues; and the unions are dialoging with environmental-justice groups around the concept. There's a lot of thinking and rethinking of the moral and theological issues of sustaining life in an ecological way. There is a direct link between all of this and brownfields. People see urban sprawl as destroying green fields and disinvesting from urban areas. The issues of value and morals are coming into the discussions. No more single-minded focus on so-called science that is devoid of social impact and values. In five years we will have an even deeper appreciation of the need for spiritual values. We need to start working with young children, get them to think and understand these connections instead of focusing on money and taxes. We need to change the terms of the debate about what constitutes a healthy and sustainable community.

Lee is distressed by the lack of urban policy in the United States and sees brownfields as a door into ecologically sensitive urban redevelopment.

> Lee: There's a crisis in America's urban areas, and there is no consistent, coherent, and concerted effort to address it. There is no real urban agenda. The urban crisis is fundamentally an ecological crisis, that is, there is a lack of integration of the natural, built, cultural, and spiritual environments. Brownfields offers real, tangible hope because there are success stories. These are rooted in the knowledge and experience and direction of the residents.
>
> The circumstances, like Chester that you intimately know, boggle the mind. People living sandwiched among refineries and other factories. It's like they don't count, don't exist. I know that some see brownfields as attempts to remove liability and clean-up standards. They see brownfields as a developer-driven construct. And in a way it is. People are trying to make a quick buck. But if the community has leadership and vision, it won't happen that way.

Charles Lee recommended Barrio Logan as a place with a vision for the future.

> Lee: In Barrio Logan the people have a vision of what a community should look like. They have the idea of a healthy and sustainable community, that is their aspiration.

At Lee's suggestion, George Dawson interviewed Diane Takvorian, Maria Moya, and Richard Juarez in the Barrio Logan neighborhood. Diane Takvorian is executive director of the Environmental Health Coalition. Maria Moya is codirector of the Toxic Free Neighborhoods Campaign and coordinator of SALTA (Salud Ambiental, Latinaes Tomando Accion, or Environmental Health, Latinos Taking Action). Richard Juarez is community development director of the San Diego Metropolitan Area Advisory Committee.

Barrio Logan

Barrio Logan is a community of approximately five square miles in the City of San Diego and has about fifty thousand residents. To the west is San Diego Bay, to the north is downtown San Diego, and to the south is National City. Ninety-five percent of the population is Latino. The neighborhood, like Chester, has multiple LULUs interspersed among residences, including a sewage-pumping station, three shipyards, two naval bases, a seaweed-processing plant, chrome-plating facilities, and chemical-storage plants. Barrio Logan is bisected north to south by a freeway, which the community strongly opposed. The *San Diego Union Tribune* has documented the presence of odors that caused evacuations from local schools and the presence of a variety of environmental hazards, including explosions, that have led to worker injuries and emergency treatments. In other words, Barrio Logan has taken more than its share of environmental hits.

> Takvorian: I'm a social worker. My background is in community organizing and advocacy. I'm not a scientist or environmentalist in terms of my training. I'm the director of the Environmental Health Coalition, and we've been at it for seventeen years in San Diego. The toxic-free neighborhood campaign is one of our oldest campaigns and reflects the kinds of actions we've taken in communities that are the most impacted by toxic pollution in San Diego. We also have a Clean Bay campaign, which encompasses the nearby military area. We also have a Border Environmental Justice Campaign that focuses on *maquiladoras* and other U.S. plants in Tijuana. That's an overview of what we do.
>
> Juarez: I'm with the Metropolitan Area Advisory Committee, which is a nonprofit, social service agency in the San Diego Metropolitan area that works on community development. The focus of my department is Barrio Logan, National City area, this particular neighborhood. We built a full block of affordable-housing units, which we will visit later, and we're working on doing a retail center here.
>
> Moya: For the last three years I've been involved with environmental issues. But I've worked in these communities for the last seven years on health-related issues.

George Dawson asked them how they became involved in environmental justice.

> Takvorian: I noticed that people seemed to be impacted by
> toxic pollution. We decided to form a group to start looking at
> these issues. I read a summary of Sam Epstein's book *The Politics
> of Cancer*.[7] It made me say, "Wow! I didn't know that all of
> these different kinds of chemicals could cause cancer." I didn't
> think of myself as naive politically. I was shocked at the
> amount of information that was being covered up. He [Epstein]
> was predominantly talking about workers. We began to realize
> how communities were being impacted. We found that a
> hazardous-waste dump was illegally put across the street from a
> school, and a block from Rich's [Juarez] house in San Diego.
> That was one of the Environmental Health Coalition's first
> projects. This was in 1981. Kids were getting sick, but nobody
> was paying attention to that. They couldn't figure out what was
> going on. One day a worker keeled over who was working on an
> abandoned lot where waste had been dumped. The kids were all
> marching through it [the lot] on the way to and from school.
> Rich and I knew each other from social service work. We
> started our efforts to get a community right-to-know law.
>
> We started organizing around getting that site cleaned up.
> You can figure out how hard that was. Nobody knew what was
> actually going on, why kids were sick, what was the relationship
> between the chemicals they finally did find on that site and the
> illnesses. That was our first foray into environmental protection
> in our neighborhood.
>
> Then there were three emergency Super Fund cleanups in
> the next few years in the same area. Part of the reason it was
> such a big deal was that homes, schools, and polluting indus-
> tries were so close to each other.
>
> Next we got a resolution passed that was never adhered to,
> that these kinds of industries, homes, and schools ought to be
> separated. The city never followed up on making the zoning
> changes or relocating the companies. In 1990, Rich essentially
> wrote an ordinance, dubbed the "Buffer-Zone Ordinance,"
> which is the heart of the *Toxic-Free Neighborhoods Community
> Planning Guide*.[8]

It was the first one proposed in the United States.

Juarez: It was never adopted. It's not even pending.

Richard Juarez described the area and highlighted the land, zoning, and environmental issues of his and many inner-city neighborhoods.

Juarez: The Barrio is intersected by Interstate Route 5 and bounded by other roadways and harbor. The area used to have many auto junk yards. These have essentially been zoned out, with a few exceptions. However, zoning has not worked well. Years ago, when the issue was smoke, noise, and lighting, zoning was written to protect people from those impacts. The zones never took chemicals into account. They can. You can have a buffer zone, or start addressing the types of chemicals that are used inside a business. We need rezoning to address today's industrial conditions.

Takvorian: Our timing was incredibly bad. We got lots of laws passed during the 1980s.

Our problem was that in the beginning of the 1990s the recession was bad. Industries were blaming everything on environmental regulation. They effectively claimed that every company in San Diego would go out of business if this buffer-zone law was passed. There was lots of rhetoric. What we did get out of it were studies and task forces. Ultimately, it [the city council] decided that plating shops and chemical supply companies should be relocated out of the community.

The MAAC [Metropolitan Areas Advisory Committee] and EHC [Environmental Health Coalition] went to EPA and said: "You've got to give them [the city] money under the brownfields program because this is an emerging brownfields. You have this polluting company [plating] which shouldn't be here. So let's do it all in one package. You move them. You clean it up. And you put a good use on it." We got EPA to buy the argument. They gave the city $100,000 so they could work on this. This gives them the money to hire staff to do a site assessment. They can pay for contractors to come in and do the assessment of how contaminated the site is. We also got the city to ante up $75,000 in community-development block-grant money to complement the EPA money. Hopefully this will be done in a year.

Charles Lee had told us that residents of brownfields neighborhoods not only needed to get more control over what was going on in their neighborhoods but had also to play a part in changing society's views. Proposition 65 was a public-initiated referendum in California that eventually led to the requirement to notify the public of chemical risks on fruits, vegetables, and other products unless risk assessments suggested the chemicals were safe. George Dawson discussed Proposition 65 with the three street fighters.

Takvorian: That was one of the first times when we realized what a strong split there was between the mainstream environmental groups and the grassroots groups. Proposition 65 was not written the way we wanted it to be written. We had a big fight about it. There are lots of loopholes in it. One of the clearest is those signs that are on every grocery store door, that say there may be chemicals inside this store that may cause cancer or reproductive effects. But there is no specificity. The hotline is essentially useless. Prop 65 didn't go far enough. In 1986, we could have gotten a lot more. The problem was that the Environmental Defense Fund and the Natural Resources Defense Council acted like they were negotiating legislation. We could have gotten more out of that bill.

Fast forward to 1990 or 1991, when the Big Green initiative came and we tried to add more than was contained in Prop 65. At that point industry was doing a really good job of saying, Environmental regulations are killing us. That was one of the first moments I realized what a big difference there is between our organization and what we lovingly call the "big ten." [The big ten refers to the largest environmental organizations.] Now they [the national environmental organizations] are claiming to have environmental-justice programs. But we don't see the evidence in terms of activity.

Nothing like Maria's SALTA project has ever come from a mainstream environmental organization. There's really no resources coming here. I think what we're proud of is that there's an intersection between planning and social services. Women are at the front of maintaining and protecting their families' health and environment.

Moya: The SALTA project is a community education program that goes into homes of families and educates them

about the problems and what to do. The main goal of SALTA is
to empower the community to act for itself. Over the last two
years we have been able to train eighteen *promotoras*. They're
health promoters, and they have educated over two hundred
people in the community. When we started this, we needed to
find out what the level of knowledge was in the community
about pollution. We started training them about the pollutants
that they might find in the home, and gradually we moved on
to other sources of pollution, until we showed them what the
pollution in the area was and the health hazards that could
result from living near these sources of pollutants.

I was provided with a set of documents distributed by SALTA
(Salud Ambiental, Latines Tomando Accion) and EHC (Environmental Health Coalition). In English and Spanish, they provide information about pollution prevention, chronic and worst-case chemicals
emissions in Barrio Logan, ideas about recycling and the toxicity of
household products, saving energy, and a variety of other safety and
health tips. The documents strike me as not written to stir up emotions and cause residents to be paranoid about every facility and prod-
uct, but rather to help people prioritize their concerns. For example,
the documents categorize land uses and activities. Health-care and food-
related facilities are characterized as of "little" or "no concern." Dry
cleaners and places where welding takes place are described as "need-
ing further study." Plating shops, sandblasting operations, chemical
manufacturing and storage, above-ground fuel storage, and ship-repair
facilities are suggested to have 1,000–foot buffer zones to the nearest
residence, school, or day care center. The third group is also suggested
to require regulatory attention, such as code enforcement. I won't say
that I agree with every bit of this classification, but I will say that I was
sufficiently impressed by it to present the EHC's classification and reasoning to my class as illustrative of the best kind of work done by a
citizens' group.

Richard Juarez observed that the EHC and SALTA have lost most
of their fights to change land use. But there have been victories.

> Moya: One of the victories we had was the methyl bromide
> fumigation plant. The Port District decided to import fruit
> [grapes] from Chile. It fumigated food as it came in, sending

fumes over the community without doing an environmental study as to what the health hazards could be. When we first started, they [the community] didn't know what this fumigant was. Now the community is well aware of what the problems may be. Through the efforts of SALTA, the people became aware of what was happening really close to their homes and near the schools. They became involved. They pushed and pushed. This last July, the Port District decided to stop bringing in any more fruit to be fumigated. It was a long effort, but we didn't get any results until the community really got involved. When we first started, only a few people came to Port meetings. The numbers kept growing. At the last one, more than 200 people attended a public meeting, listened, and testified. Now we're working with the community on relocating some of those plating shops and chemical warehouses.

Diane Takvorian emphasized that their focus was on all environmental hazards, not just the obvious ones like a fumigant plant.

Takvorian: There are many factories around here that are out of code. If we go out to one of these places at 8 o'clock at night you can hear the noise. That's something we can all understand. It's not some invisible stuff coming over that you can't see or smell. But the code-compliance people won't do anything about it. That's where the SALTA project is so important because all these women are now empowered, and know whom you should call, and how many times you have to call, so action on many things is starting to happen.

While I have focused on the anticontamination theme that is a cornerstone of Barrio Logan's program, the community leaders are engaged in a full range of efforts to fight crime, rebuild housing, and provide social services. For example, Diane Takvorian, Maria Moya, Richard Juarez, and Francisca Jimenez (*la promotora*) took George Dawson on a tour of the neighborhood. They visited the Mercado Apartments, which Juarez arranged to have built with federal tax credits and Bank of America financing. The apartments are 144 units, mostly two and three bedrooms. George Dawson was impressed by the cleanliness of the area, especially of Chicano Park, and the beautiful murals painted all over the neighborhood. Forty of the murals drawn by community members are on the pillars that hold up the Coronado Bridge. Some depict an antipollution theme. These are not graffiti; they are art—beautiful, expressive art drawn on structures that symbolize the former powerlessness of the neighborhood.

Charles Lee was right when he suggested that the community leaders had a vision that integrated environmental justice and ecologically sensitive land use. Here are the six principles underlying their vision of a toxic-free neighborhood presented in their community guide to planning.[9]

1. Residents of every community are equally entitled to protection from exposure to toxic materials.
2. Dangerous amounts of hazardous materials should not be stored, used, or released in or adjacent to residential neighborhoods.
3. Planning and zoning regulations should ensure that future land uses are compatible.
4. The level of toxics protection should be adequate to safeguard society's most vulnerable members: children, the elderly, the sick, and pregnant or nursing women.
5. Businesses create vitality in neighborhoods and deserve support. Technical assistance for toxics-use reduction should be provided to businesses whose emissions or accident potential may threaten the public health. Economic assistance should be provided to aid businesses in relocating to more suitable locations within the community when toxics-use reduction is not possible.
6. Local governments must promote economic development and land uses that enhance neighborhoods, including the identification and recruitment of environmentally responsible businesses. Priority should be given to maintaining San Diego's manufacturing base and worker representation.

These six principles, the newsletters and other educational programs, and an organization with over two thousand members are evidence that these street fighters have lived in and cared about this community for years. Yet the published academic literature suggests that neighborhood leadership is hard to sustain in poor neighborhoods. Barrio Logan is obviously a striking exception. George Dawson concluded his interviews by asking Diane Takvorian, Richard Juarez, and Maria

Moya to react to the literature's low expectations of leadership in poor neighborhoods.

> Juarez: I've been involved in this community for more than twenty years. It is my backyard. There's nowhere to go. I can leave, but my grandparents are still here. My cousins are still here. At some point you realize, Yeah, my life can be better. I can ignore this and not have this headache. But the conditions have not changed. Those conditions need to change.
>
> Moya: There needs to be someone working to help people make changes. If we all turn our backs, things would be worse. It is very rewarding. That's what pulled me into this issue. It's trying to make the lives of other people a little bit better, trying to help people as much as I can.
>
> Takvorian: It's part of our obligation as members of a community. What's the alternative? I mean, for me, the integration between civil rights and environmental quality was pretty clear. For me personally, I guess the question is, What's the alternative? It is incredibly gratifying to work with people in the community, like the ones Rich and Maria have been describing. People want to make their lives better. They just don't have the information. An organization that can get information to people so that they change their neighborhoods makes a huge difference.

Juarez summarized their collective view:

> This effort to improve the community has been going on for twenty years. About twenty years ago, there was an organized effort at community planning. What do people want? There was a community-improvement study commissioned by the city. A vision was created of what should be done in the future. People from the neighborhood went to the city council, the planning commission, to get these plans approved. There were a lot of battles. Jump forward to where we are now. We have a youth-training program, a youth program, we hire neighborhood kids to train them in the building trades. These kids worked on our apartment project. They told us a story of them remembering their mothers dragging them to those meetings [twenty years ago] where their mothers were fighting for

changes in the community. Now these kids feel like it is their turn to do something for the community. The next generation is actually building the houses their mothers were fighting for.

Accomplishments

What Charles Lee, Ben Chavis, Leon White, Charles Cobb, and others started in North Carolina has forced government, science, and business to consider environmental hazards, land use, and neighborhood quality. Scientists and other technical experts can no longer dismiss irate residents of inner-city and poor rural neighborhoods as uninformed, irrational people suffering from paranoia and manipulated by outside agitators. It is obvious that residents of environmentally stressed neighborhoods such as those in Chester, San Diego, and Rahway are increasing their information base and are able to legally and politically challenge cavalier and biased science. For example, it is embarrassing, or should be embarrassing, to EPA and academic scientists not to be able to discuss cumulative impacts of pollutants in cities.

The environmental-justice movement has reinvigorated those who believe that we need to link the built, natural, social, and spiritual environments when we develop neighborhoods rather than continue to permit fragmented land-use decision making. I hear planners, developers, and others talk about holistic designs, livable neighborhoods, and working with the residents rather than resetting cookie-cutter neighborhoods all over the landscape. In inner cities, people recognize that we can't separate economic blight and environmental blight. With respect to business, the environmental-justice movement has focused on preventing pollution instead of burying or burning waste products. Some businesses have fought against pollution prevention. Yet, in general, businesses have embraced pollution prevention to the extent that they are saving money formerly spent on raw materials and waste treatment, and some are marketing their pollution-prevention methods.

The most important accomplishment of the grassroots environmental-justice movement is the creation of some neighborhoods that can fight powerful economic and political interests. These communities have developed methods of communications and research that are culturally sensitive and empowering. They have learned how to go from site-specific struggles about LULUs to community-wide visions and planning. They have learned how to link environmental restoration, economic revitalization, and neighborhood quality. These neighborhoods will survive the neighborhood triage going on in the United States. The challenge to those who believe in the ideas of environmental justice and sustainable neighborhoods is how to help create and support more leaders who can help their neighborhoods survive and prosper.

Epilogue

THE FIRST SET of interviews for this book occurred in 1996. Curiosity got the best of me, so all the street fighters were called in July and August of 1998.

Yvonne Carrington's efforts described in chapter 2 have continued.

> Carrington: We have come a long way since you came down to interview me, and things have improved substantially. We are involved with fifty or so more programs. I feel that I'm better educated because I now have more experience and training. I understand things more. Regarding housing, the Ruth Bennett Homes have been completely renovated. The homes are quite beautiful now. But we still must deal with little problems that are being taken care of. We are not yet completely independent, but we are off the troubled list. I would say that we've moved from 40 percent to 78 percent independent. However, we will be not be fully independent until other housing projects in the city are renovated. In order to emphasize that the Homes have changed, we will change the name to "'Bennett Estates" or to "Bennett Terrace."

Other programs have also been born at the Bennett Homes.

> Carrington: I'm particularly happy that there are more programs for the kids, such as involving the kids in a tee-shirt-

making business. We now have a program for teenagers emphasizing abstinence. Our latest "success story" was a girl with two children who graduated Chester High with honors and has two jobs. In fact, we just started a program for young ladies who get pregnant. We have literally "saved" twenty to twenty-five of these young kids. We just had a Community United Day two Thursdays ago, and we are trying to get the message across that we will not tolerate drugs. We have been strictly enforcing the "one strike you're out" policy in the Homes. We also have a tenant patrol for dealing with the drug problem. I am particularly impressed that many people are helping out, and nobody seems to be afraid to give names. There certainly is a more positive feeling, as we are becoming more independent.

Personally, I am feeling a little burnt out. Right now, I am trying to get other people organized so they will eventually be able to take care of things. However, we still have a long way to go, especially in terms of those people who just do not realize that welfare reform is here to stay.

On August 17, 1998, the Carringtons remembered Carla's tragic death with a special celebration at the parking lot where Carla had been killed.

I was not surprised to find that Reverend Garlic (chapter 3) had not retired and was working on drug-related crime, housing, and employment.

Garlic: The drug problem is definitely not as visible as it once was, but it remains a problem we must continue to work on every day. The employment level is about the same, but we are starting new programs to help people get jobs. For instance, we now have a "one stop service center" so people can get help, and we are offering more employment training. In fact, we just opened a computer training center. I have been just as busy as ever, but I hope to retire at the end of the year.

Jennifer and David Knowlton are in contact with their friends at Neah Bay (chapter 4).

Jennifer: They've gotten more grants to build the environmental department. And they have been invited to apply for the funds to build a modern marina office that will replace the existing temporary one you saw. It will be the command center for the marina, for the port, and for training everyone associated with the marina. It is the last piece of the puzzle. I feel so good for the tribe.

The Knowltons are slowly adjusting to Eugene, Oregon. David is able to focus on patient care, which he enjoys, and he no longer has to worry every time he hears a siren go off. But the Knowltons miss Neah Bay.

> Jennifer: We spend so much time consuming here that we don't spend as much time building good relationships with people the way we did at Neah Bay. We've joined a parents group and other groups to try to re-create some of the nurturing environment of Neah Bay. I wish Ben had been born and lived in Neah Bay for at least a few years. It would have been good for him.

Ann Parker (chapter 5) was frank about what is going on in the neighborhood.

> Parker: As you know, the incinerator is up and running. I'm just quite disappointed and disheartened about the whole situation. I'm filled with a sense of doubt. I haven't been active in the group lately, as I have had very urgent family matters to deal with. However, the others have been more active.

Kerri Blanchard provided more details:

> Blanchard: The bad news is the incinerator. When the flow-control restrictions were declared illegal, the utilities authority had to drop the tipping fee price to $50 a ton to keep their customers. They lost tens of thousands of dollars a day. They are still not getting enough garbage to fully utilize and pay off the incinerator. They are talking about burning non-garbage at the facility. We are worried about the impact of whatever else they burn. The second bad news is that a medical-waste destruction plant is being considered for a site about a quarter mile down the road from here.

The good news for the neighborhood is the former GAF site, where the commercial hazardous-waste incinerator was to be located.

Blanchard: International Specialty Products [the former GAF],
which was going to build the commercial hazardous-waste
incinerator at Tremley Point, has agreed to seek an alternative
use for the site.

Kerri, however, remains skeptical. Well over a million dollars has been
spent in legal fees, fighting the application for the commercial hazardous-
waste incinerator.

Blanchard: At least they can stop fighting each other in court
for a while. But the state has to agree that the commercial
hazardous-waste incinerator is no longer required, and the
company has to find another profitable use for the site.

In other words, the neighborhood remains at risk for additional LULUs.
The incinerator bond default issue has been temporarily solved. In November 1998, New Jersey taxpayers voted in favor of a bond issue that
pays much of the bond debt.

There is also good and sad news from Detroit's arson squad (chapter 6). Chief Peck of the arson squad retired in June 1998. Captain
Bozich was promoted to chief of the arson squad. And Jim Bush is now
executive fire chief of the City of Detroit. Even though the arson squad
is still composed of twenty-four positions, Chief Bozich feels that the
promotion of Jim Bush is another illustration that the Archer administration is focusing on arson.

Bozich: Some tactical changes are being made for our Devil's
Night efforts, including moving our temporary headquarters to
a more convenient location and recruiting many more volunteers. The International Association of Arson Investigators [the
premier international anti-arson organizations] has just voted to
give Detroit's arson squad the "Superior Achievement Award,"
which is only given out to one squad a year. This is awarded to
the arson unit displaying the best tactics and techniques in
fighting arson, and we're quite proud of this great achievement.

But not all the news from Detroit was good.

Bozich: Our squad's workload has increased significantly. This
past year the frequency of arson occurrences has remained
pretty static. However, there has been a noticeable increase in

arson-related fatalities, which most probably is just a cyclical phenomenon. In fact, this year the first half of the year had more fatalities than in all of last year. These fatalities have caused us to spend a great deal more time in court, away from the street. Regarding the Roland Waters arson-murder, we are now teaming up with the television program "America's Most Wanted" to try to track down this third killer, who skipped bail and is still on the run.

Phil Kirk updated me on FEMA's recent efforts in the Midwest (chapter 7).

Kirk: There has been no disaster that our FEMA branch was involved with comparable to the floods of 1993. We have recently been devoting a great deal of time to the consequences of the recent grain-elevator explosion in Kansas. The DeBruce Grain Company elevator was the third largest in the world, and it was a significant disaster. At least five people were killed. Right now it is much too early to determine the consequences of this disaster and for our agency to figure out how to deal with it in the long run.

In terms of other projects, we are excited about our FEMA-initiated Project Impact, the focus of which is to help build disaster-resistant communities. In this effort, one community per state is designated a prime example of a disaster-resistant community. [The disaster-resistant community in New Jersey is Trenton.] We have put a lot of time and resources into this project, and I feel this shows how FEMA has moved in the direction of prevention as indicated in your chapter.

At the beginning of chapter 7, I pronounced Pattonsburg dead. I was wrong. For a few weeks in May 1998, it came alive again. The old town was purchased to film Director Ang Lee's $35-million film *Ride With the Devil*, a Civil War drama based on an attack on Lawrence, Kansas, by Confederate guerillas under William Clark Quantrill. Designers spent three months covering concrete, removing telephone poles, and adding new buildings. In short, Pattonsburg, made over to look like a mid-nineteenth-century midwestern town, will live a new life on film. MCA/Universal studios expects to release the film before the end of 1998.

Trenton, New Jersey, continues to earn kudos for its innovative economic development programs (chapter 8).

> Alan Mallach: We have received a lot of federal recognition. We are one of six places to get Home Ownership Zone grants from HUD. We have been selected as one of sixteen cities by the U.S. Environmental Protection Agency to demonstrate brownfields redevelopment. Our regional economy has been steadily improving-income There has been more investment and more development interest, especially by industrial and distribution firms. Employment in Trenton has improved. In fact, our unemployment rate is under double digits for the first time in over a decade. Also, major developers are now looking to develop in the waterfront area, and even in downtown, as well. Mayor Palmer was just re-elected a month ago, and he received an overwhelming 87 percent of the vote. Obviously, this shows that many people here think that we're moving in the right direction and things are picking up.
>   However, some projects happen faster than others. The arena is under construction and the hotel project is close to being complete. Unfortunately, the Champale project just isn't getting off the ground as rapidly as I had hoped. The other brownfields sites are proving to be tougher to market to developers. I'm working hard and trying to be patient.

Charles Lee is excited about the impact of the environmental-justice movement. Most recently, using the provisions of Title VI of the Civil Rights Act of 1964, a number of lawsuits, including one in Chester, have challenged the right to locate LULUs in already heavily burdened minority neighborhoods. The U.S. Environmental Protection Agency has developed a policy that asserts its right to hold up or deny an application that violates environmental-justice guidelines. Charles Lee acknowledges that the EPA guidance documents may not have been justified in some instances, but that the net result is that we have been forced to confront the interaction of civil rights, employment, and public health. At least ten states—including Maryland, New Jersey, New York, Pennsylvania, Oregon, and Texas—are explicitly considering environmental-justice policies. This is forcing the states to talk with the local jurisdictions. While some are working hard behind the scenes to change the policy, many states are saying, Let's get on with a solution instead of complaining.

Lee is a member of the Title VI Federal Advisory Committee to the EPA. He hopes to spend a good deal of time focusing on how government can be changed to be more responsive to people's sometimes desperate needs. Title VI he views as illustrative of how important government can be to neighborhoods.

> Lee: I have seen the benefits that government action can have on people's quality of life and neighborhood quality. Changing the neighborhood, helping them out of hideous environmental conditions, helps motivate the people to change themselves, to improve their lives. It gives them hope.

Notes

Chapter 1 Neighborhood Quality and Street Fighters

1. M. R. Greenberg and D. Schneider, *Environmentally Devastated Neighborhoods: Perceptions, Policies, and Realities* (New Brunswick, N.J.: Rutgers University Press, 1996). The best historical data set on neighborhoods is maintained by the U.S. Department of Commerce (*American Housing Survey for the United States: 1993* [Washington, D.C.: U.S. Government Printing Office, 1994]). There is a good deal of literature on the factors that lead to good neighborhoods and the importance of neighborhoods. See S. Aitken, "Local Evaluation of Neighborhood Change," *Annals of Association of American Geographers* 80 (1990): 247–267; W. Gallagher, *The Power of Place: How Our Surroundings Shape Our Thoughts, Emotions, and Actions* (New York: Poseidon Press, 1993); and P. Clay and R. Hollister, eds. *Neighborhood Policy and Planning* (Lexington, Mass.: Lexington Books, 1983). However, please note that neighborhood is only one of many characteristics that influence the quality of life. See A. Campbell, P. Converse, and W. Rodgers, *The Quality of American Life: Perceptions, Evaluations, and Satisfactions* (New York: Russell Sage Foundation, 1976), for an early (but still the best) review of factors influencing quality of life, including the local environment.

2. See M. R. Greenberg, "Understanding the Civic Activities of the Residents of Inner City Neighborhoods: Two Case Studies," *Urban Geography* 19 (1998): 68–76, and M. R. Greenberg and D. Schneider, "Neighborhood Quality, Environmental Hazards, Personal Traits, and Resident Actions," *Risk Analysis* 17 (1997): 169–175. See also M. Edelstein, *Contaminated Communities: The Social and Psychological Impacts of Residential Toxic Exposures* (Boulder, Colo.: Westview Press, 1983); L. Friedman, D. Nelson, P. Baer, M. Lane, P. Smith, et al., "The Relationship of Dispositional Optimism, Daily Life Stress, and Domestic Environment to Coping Methods Used by Cancer Patients," *Journal of Behavioral Medicine* 15 (1992): 127–141; A. Furnham and H. Steele, "Measuring Locus of Control: A Critique of General, Children's, Health-Work-Related Locus of Control Questionnaires," *British Journal of Psychology* 84 (1993): 443–479; E. Lin and C. Peterson, "Pessimistic Explanatory Style and Response to Illness," *Behavioral Research and Therapy* 28 (1990): 243–248.

3. M. Lewis, "No Relief from Politics: Machine Bosses and Civil Works, *Urban Affairs Quarterly* 30 (1994): 210–213. See also D. Judd, *The Politics of American Cities* (Glenview, Ill.: Scott, Foresman, Inc., 1988); and G. Pomper, ed., *The Election of 1984: Reports and Interpretations* (Chatham, N.J.: Chatham House, 1984).

4. J. Galbraith, *The Culture of Contentment* (New York: Houghton Mifflin, Co., 1992); S. Fainstein and A. Markusen, "The Urban Policy Challenge: Integrating Across Social and Economic Development Policy," *North Carolina Law Review* 71 (1993): 1463–1486; and M. Gottdiener, "What Ever Happened to the Urban Crisis," *Urban Affairs Quarterly* 20 (1985): 421–427.

5. R. Putnam, "The Strange Disappearance of Civic America," *The American Prospect* 24 (1996): 34–48.

6. J. Leavitt and S. Saegert, "The Community Household: Responding to Housing Abandonment in New York City," *APA Journal* autumn 1988, pp. 489–500. For an encouraging perspective on how to get people and institutions to work together, see L. Schorr, *Within Our Reach: Breaking the Cycle of Disadvantage* (New York: Anchor Books, Doubleday, 1988), and its follow-up, L. Schorr, *Common Purpose: Strengthening Families and Neighborhoods to Build America* (New York: Anchor Books, Doubleday, 1997).

7. Greenberg, "Understanding the Civic Activities of the Residents"; M. R. Greenberg; "High-Rise Public Housing, Optimism, and Personal Environmental Health Behaviors," *American Journal of Health Behavior* 21 (1997): 387–398.

8. Tying neighborhood activism to trust and personality characteristics was a new finding. However, these behaviors and personality characteristics have been observed in behaviors related to personal public health behaviors and in reaction to environmental risks. See M. Baldassare and C. Katz, "The Personal Threat of Environmental Problems as Predictor of Environmental Practices," *Environment and Behavior* 24 (1992): 602–616; Clay and Hollister, *Neighborhood Policy and Planning*; J. Flynn, W. Burns, C. Mertz, and P. Slovic, "Trust as a Determinant of Opposition to a High-Level Radioactive Waste Depository: Analysis of a Structural Model," *Risk Analysis* 12 (1992): 417–429; N. Freudenberg and C. Steinsapir, "Not in Our Backyards: The Grassroots Environmental Movement," *Society and Natural Resources* 4 (1991): 235–245; S. Miller, M. Rein, and P. Levitt, "Community Action in the United States," *Community Development Journal* 25 (1990): 356–368; Friedman, et al., "The Relationship of Dispositional Optimism"; Furnham and Steele, "Measuring Locus of Control"; and Lin and Peterson, "Pessimistic Explanatory Style and Response to Illness."

9. D. Monti, *Race, Redevelopment, and the New Company Towns* (Albany: State University of New York Press, 1990).

10. A. Garvin, *The American City: What Works, What Doesn't* (New York: McGraw-Hill, 1996). See also T. Clark, *Urban Innovation* (Thousand Oaks, Calif.: Sage, 1994); J. Luke, *Catalytic Leadership: Strategies for an Interconnected World* (San Francisco: Jossey-Bass Publishers, 1997); D. Osborne and T. Gaebler, *Reinventing Government* (Reading, Mass.: Addison-Wesley, 1992); and J. Wilson, *Bureaucracy: What Government Agencies Do and Why They Do It* (New York: Basic Books, 1989).

11. An excellent example is in housing. See L. Keyes, A. Schwartz, A. Vidal, and R. Bratt, "Networks and Nonprofits: Opportunities and Challenges in an Era of Federal Devolution," *Housing Policy Debate* 7 (1996): 201–229.

12. Grogan, quoted in "Civic Environmentalism," newsletter of the National Commission on Civic Renewal (College Park: University of Maryland, 1996), 2.

13. R. Gittell, *Renewing Cities* (Princeton, N.J.: Princeton University Press, 1992), 157.

14. D. Moynihan, *Miles to Go: A Personal History of Social Policy Change* (Cambridge, Mass.: Harvard University Press, 1996).

15. M. Stegman, "Federal Urban Policy and the Budget," *CUP Report* 7 (1996): 1 and 3.
16. M. Orfield, *Metropolitics: A Regional Agenda for Community and Stability* (Washington, D.C.: The Brookings Institution, 1997). See also A. Downs, *New Visions for Metropolitan America* (Washington, D.C.: The Brookings Institution and Lincoln Institute of Land Policy, 1994).

Chapter 2 Life From Death: Public Housing in Chester

1. M. Janofsky, "Residents Reclaim Their Old Way of Life," *New York Times*, 14 August 1996, p. 10.
2. D. Hardy, "Tenants Have a Stake in Bennett Homes," *Philadelphia Inquirer*, 21 August 1995, p. w7.
3. Greenberg and Schneider, *Environmentally Devastated Neighborhoods*, 79–108.
4. There is a large and readable literature on this subject. For example, D. Massey and N. Denton, *American Apartheid* (Cambridge, Mass.: Harvard University Press, 1991), and A. Kotlowitz, *There Are No Children Here* (New York: Anchor Books, 1991). For more recent papers on the evolving controversy about concentrating and dispersing low-income populations, see P. Dreir, "Philanthropy and the Housing Crisis," *Housing Policy Debate* 8 (1997): 235–293; J. Kasarda and K.-W. Ting, "Joblessness and Poverty in America's Central Cities: Causes and Policy Prescriptions," *Housing Policy Debate* 7 (1996): 387–419; W. Rohe and R. Kleit, "From Dependency to Self-Sufficiency: An Appraisal of the Gateway Transitional Families Program," *Housing Policy Debate* 8 (1997): 75–108; and L. Picus, "Current Issues in Public Urban Education," *Housing Policy Debate* 7 (1996): 715–729.
5. M. R. Greenberg, D. Schneider, J. Moskowitz, and L. Duncan, "Putting the Public Back Into Public Health," *New Jersey Medicine*, August (1998): 45–50.
6. Janofsky, "Residents Reclaim Their Old Way of Life."
7. S. Venkatesh, "An Invisible Community. Inside Chicago's Public Housing," *The American Prospect* 34 (September–October 1997): 35–40. See also comments and replies in *The American Prospect* 35 (November–December 1997): 12–13 and 93.

Chapter 3 Joseph Garlic: Planting Seeds of Hope in Elizabethport

1. M. Brown, *Laying Waste: The Poisoning of America by Toxic Chemical* (New York: Washington Square Press, 1981), 159.
2. L. Peterson, "Work Is Underway on Housing Projects," *Star Ledger* (Newark), 26 April 1991, p. 33.
3. S. Lovell, "Brand New Housing," *Star Ledger* (Newark), 22 July 1994, p. 25.
4. S. Lovell, "Home New Home," *Star Ledger* (Newark), 8 May 1996, p. 23.
5. L. Peterson, "Community Pride: Elizabethport Plans Day of Unity and Fun," *Star Ledger* (Newark) 17 April 1991, p. 29.

Chapter 4 Neah Bay: Forward to the Past

1. F. Mullen, *Plagues and Politics: The Story of the United States Public Health Service* (New York: Basic Books, 1989).
2. National Center for Health Statistics, *Health, United States, 1995* (Hyattsville, Md.: Public Health Service, 1996).

3. S. Coleman, *Physician Distribution and Rural Access to Medical Services: Executive Summary* (Santa Monica, Calif.: Rand Corporation, for the DHEW, 1976).

4. W. Gessler and T. Ricketts, eds., *Health in Rural North America* (New Brunswick, N.J.: Rutgers University Press, 1992).

5. S. Baker, R. Whitfield, and B. O'Neill, "Geographic Variations in Mortality from Motor Vehicle Crashes," *New England Journal of Medicine* 316 (1987): 1384–1387.

6. M. Parker Pascua, "Ozette: A Makah Village in 1491," *National Geographic* October 1991, pp. 38–43.

7. Ibid., 40.

Chapter 5   Ground Zero: Concerned Citizens Fight Against Massive Poison Machines

1. J. Bailey, "Economics of Trash," *Wall Street Journal*, 3 December 1991, pp. A1 and A9.

2. J. Picard, "Turnpike Oks Burner Plan," *The Home News & Tribune*, 24 December 1996, p.1.

Chapter 6   Detroit's Arson Squad: Taking Back Neighborhoods from Fire

1. K. Bryant, Comcast Cablevision of Detroit, 18 October 1996, 2 pages.

2. P. Waldmeir, "Take a Bow Mr. Mayor for Snuffing Out Devil's Night Fires," *The Detroit News*, 3 November 1995, p.3. For a very different view of the role of government in neighborhoods, see R. Wallace, "Homelessness, Contagious Destruction of Housing and Municipal Service Cuts in New York City: Demographics of Housing Deficit," *Environment and Planning* 21 (1989): 1585–1603.

3. S. Hackney, "Archer Warns Detroit to Be Vigilant for Devil's Night," *The Detroit News*, 24 September 1996, p. 1.

4. "Do You Think Detroiters Will Continue to Reduce the Fires on Devil's Night," *The Detroit News*, 3 October 1996, p. D1.

5. Press release by the City of Detroit, 1 November 1996. See also "Urban Community Intervention to Prevent Halloween Arson -Detroit, Michigan, 1985–1996," *MMWR* 46 (1997): 299–304.

6. S. Hackney, "Archer on Winning Streak: Success Over Devil's Night Gives Detroit Another Reason to Be Proud," *The Detroit News*, 3 November 1996, p. B2.

7. Ibid.

8. S. Hackney, "Devil's Night: Crusaders Make Year-Round Effort at Safety," *The Detroit News*, 23 October 1996, p. 1.

9. U.S. Fire Administration, Federal Emergency Management Agency, Emergency News Service—ENN Daily Report, 5 May 1996, from World-Wide Web Site.

10. "Vision of Detroit," 1996, a one-page handout distributed by Michelle Zdrodowski, senior publicist, City of Detroit.

11. Hackney, "Archer on Winning Streak." See also the text of the State of the City Address, 28 January 1997.

Chapter 7 Coping With and Preventing Disasters: The Federal Emergency Management Agency

1. Interagency Floodplain Management Review Committee, Scientific Assessment and Strategy Team to the Administration Floodplain Management Task Force, *Science for Floodplain Management Into the 21st Century, a Blueprint for Change* (Washington, D.C.: FEMA, 1994); State Emergency Management Agency, Missouri, *Out of Harm's Way, The Missouri Buy Out Program* (Jefferson City, Mo.: SEMA, 1995); State Emergency Management Agency, Missouri, *The Response, Recovery and Lessons Learned from the Missouri Floods of 1993 and 1994* (Jefferson City, Mo.: SEMA, 1994).
2. Interagency Floodplain Management Review Committee, *Science for Floodplain Management.*
3. J. Barry, *Rising Tide: The Great Mississippi Flood of 1927 and How It Changed America* (Indianapolis, Ind.: MacMillan Publishing, 1997).
4. E. Krug, M-J. Kresnow, J. Peddicord, L. Dahlberg, K. Powell, A. Crosby, and J. Annest, "Suicide After Natural Disasters," *New England Journal of Medicine* 338 (1998): 373–378.
5. Interagency Floodplain Management Review Committee, *Science for Floodplain Management.*
6. Ibid.
7. Ibid., vii.
8. State Emergency Management Agency, *Out of Harm's Way,* 14. See also Governor's Task Force on Flood Plain Management, *Report and Recommendations* (Jefferson City, Mo.: SEMA, July 1994); and State Emergency Management Agency, Missouri, *After Action Report, the 1995 Missouri Flood* (Jefferson City, Mo.: SEMA, 1995).
9. Interagency Floodplain Management Review Committee, *Science for Floodplain Management.*
10. State Emergency Management Agency, *Out of Harm's Way,* 9.
11. Ibid., 10.
12. Ibid., 4.
13. Ibid., 2.
14. Ibid., 11.
15. Federal Emergency Management Agency, *Strategic Plan: Partnership for a Safer Future* (Washington, D.C.: FEMA, 1997), 56. See also the review of FEMA's plan: General Accounting Office, *Results Act: Observations on the Federal Emergency Management Agency's Draft Strategic Plan* (Washington, D.C.: GAO/RCED-97-204R, 1997), 14.
16. There is a growing body of literature on this subject. See, for example, S. Dalby, "Ecological Discourse: Environmental Security and Political Geography," *Progress in Human Geography* 16 (1992): 503–522; N. Lewis and J. Mayer, "Disease as a Natural Hazard," *Progress in Human Geography* 12 (1988): 15–33; and I. Sachs, "Vulnerability of Giant Cities and the Life Lottery" in *The Metropolis Era,* ed. M. Dogan and J. Kasarda, 1:337–350 (Newbury Park, Calif.: Sage Publications, 1988).
17. E. Noji, ed., *The Public Health Consequences of Disasters* (New York: Oxford University Press, 1997).

Chapter 8   *Planning for Love of Justice*

1. D. Kirp, J. Dwyer, and L. Rosenthal, *Our Town: Race, Housing and the Soul of Suburbia* (New Brunswick, N.J.: Rutgers University Press, 1995).
2. A. Mallach, *Inclusionary Housing Programs: Policies and Practices* (New Brunswick, N.J.: Center for Urban Policy Research, Rutgers University, 1984).
3. See N. Calavita, K. Grimes, and A. Mallach, "Inclusionary Housing in California and New Jersey: A Comparative Analysis," *Housing Policy Debate* 8 (1997): 109–142; R. Burchell, D. Listokin, and A. Pashman, *Regional Housing Opportunities for Lower-Income Households* (Washington, D.C.: U.S. Department of Housing and Urban Development, 1994); and Kirp, Dwyer, and Rosenthal, *Our Town.*
4. M. R. Greenberg, F. Popper, and B. West, "TOADS: A New American Urban Epidemic," *Urban Affairs Quarterly* 25(1990): 438–457.
5. Department of Housing and Development, *Trenton: A Brownfields Showcase Community* (Trenton, N.J.: Department of Housing and Development, 1997).

Chapter 9   *A Vision of Environmental Justice and Sustainable Neighborhoods*

1. Commission for Racial Justice, United Church of Christ, *Toxic Wastes and Race in the United States: A National Report on the Racial and Socioeconomic Characteristics of Communities with Hazardous Waste Sites* (Washington, D.C.: United Church of Christ, 1987). There is a large and controversial literature about environmental equity and racism. See, for example, D. Anderton, A. Anderson, J. Oakes, and M. Fraser, "Environmental Equity: The Demographics of Dumping," *Demography* 31 (1994): 229–248; V. Been, "Locally Undesirable Land Uses in Minority Neighborhoods: Disproportionate Siting or Market Dynamics?" *The Yale University Law Review* 103 (1994): 1383–1422; B. Bryant and P. Mohai, eds., *Race and Incidence of Environmental Hazards: A Time for Discourse* (Boulder, Colo.: Westview Press, 1992); R. Bullard, *Dumping on Dixie: Race, Class, and Environmental Quality* (Boulder, Colo.: Westview Press, 1990); M. Gerrard, *Whose Backyard, Whose Risk: Fear and Fairness in Toxic and Nuclear Waste Siting* (Cambridge, Mass.: MIT Press, 1994); M. R. Greenberg and M. Cidon, "Broadening the Definition of Environmental Equity: A Framework for States and Local Governments," *Population Research and Policy Review* 16 (1997): 397–413; and R. Zimmerman, "Social Equity and Environmental Risk," *Risk Analysis* 13 (1993): 649–666.
2. M. Meadows, "Environmental Justice? Landfill Prompts Concern in North Carolina," in *Closing the Gap* (Washington, D.C.: Office of Minority Health, Public Health Service, USHHS, October 1997), 2.
3. Ibid.
4. Ibid.
5. Ibid.
6. Ibid.
7. S. Epstein, *The Politics of Cancer* (New York: Garden City Press, 1979).
8. Environmental Health Coalition, *Toxic-Free Neighborhoods Community Planning Guide* (San Diego, Calif.: Environmental Health Coalition, 1993).
9. Ibid.

Selected Bibliography

Bryant, B., and P. Mohai, eds. *Race and Incidence of Environmental Hazards: A Time for Discourse*. Boulder, Colo.: Westview Press, 1992.

Bullard, B. *Dumping on Dixie: Race, Class, and Environmental Quality*. Boulder, Colo.: Westview Press, 1990.

Campbell, A., P. Converse, and W. Rodgers. *The Quality of American Life: Perceptions, Evaluations, and Satisfactions*. New York: Russell Sage Foundation, 1976.

Clark, T. *Urban Innovation*. Thousand Oaks, Calif.: Sage Publications, 1994.

Clay, P., and R. Hollister, eds. *Neighborhood Policy and Planning*. Lexington, Mass.: Lexington Books, 1983.

Commission for Racial Justice, United Church of Christ. *Toxic Wastes and Race in the United States: A National Report on the Racial and Socioeconomic Characteristics of Communities with Hazardous Waste Sites*. Washington, D.C.: United Church of Christ, 1987.

Committee for Economic Development. *Rebuilding Inner City Communities: A New Approach to the Nation's Urban Crisis*. New York: Committee for Economic Development, 1995.

Downs, A. *New Visions for Metropolitan America*. Washington, D.C.: The Brookings Institution and Lincoln Institute of Land Policy, 1994.

Drucker, P. *The New Realities*. New York: Harper & Row, 1989.

Edelstein, M. *Contaminated Communities: The Social and Psychological Impacts of Residential Toxic Exposures*. Boulder, Colo.: Westview Press, 1983.

Galbraith, J. *The Culture of Contentment*. New York: Houghton Mifflin Co., 1992.

Gallagher, W. *The Power of Place: How Our Surroundings Shape Our Thoughts, Emotions, and Actions*. New York: Poseidon Press, 1993.

Garvin, A. *The American City: What Works, What Doesn't*. New York: McGraw-Hill, 1996.

Gerrard, M. *Whose Backyard, Whose Risk: Fear and Fairness in Toxic and Nuclear Waste Siting*. Cambridge, Mass.: MIT Press, 1994.

Gittell, R. *Renewing Cities*. Princeton, N.J.: Princeton University Press, 1992.

Greenberg, M. R., and D. Schneider. *Environmentally Devastated Neighborhoods: Perceptions, Policies, and Realities*. New Brunswick, N.J.: Rutgers University Press, 1996.

Interagency Floodplain Management Review Committee, Scientific Assessment and Strategy Team to the Administration Floodplain Management Task Force. *Science for Floodplain Management into the 21st Century, a Blueprint for Change*. Washington, D.C.: FEMA, 1994.

Jakle, J., and D. Wilson. *Derelict Landscapes: The Wasting Away of America's Built Environment*. New York: Vintage Books, 1992.

Judd, D. *The Politics of American Cities*. 3rd ed. Glenview, Ill.: Scott, Foresman, Inc., 1988.

Kotlowitz, A. *There Are No Children Here*. New York: Anchor Books, 1991.

Kozol, J. *Savage Inequalities: Children and Americans' Schools*. New York: Harper Perennial, 1991.

Luke, J. *Catalytic Leadership: Strategies for an Interconnected World*. San Francisco: Jossey-Bass Publishers, 1997.

Massey, D., and N. Denton. *American Apartheid*, Cambridge, Mass.: Harvard University Press, 1991.

Medoff, P., and H. Sklar. *Streets of Hope: The Fall and Rise of an Urban Neighborhood*. Boston: South End Press, 1994.

Moynihan, D. *Miles to Go: A Personal History of Social Policy*. Cambridge, Mass.: Harvard University Press, 1996.

Noji, E., ed. *The Public Health Consequences of Disasters*. New York: Oxford University Press, 1997.

Orfield, M. *Metropolitics: A Regional Agenda for Community and Stability*. Washington, D.C.: The Brookings Institution, 1997.

Osborne, D., and T. Gaebler. *Reinventing Government*. Reading, Mass.: Addison-Wesley, 1992.

Piller, D. *The Fail-Safe Society: Community Defiance and the End of American Technological Optimism*. Berkeley and Los Angeles: University of California Press, 1991.

Rose, H., and P. McClain. *Race, Place, and Risk: Black Homicide in Urban America*. Albany: State University of New York Press, 1990.

Rosenberg, M., and M. Fenley., eds. *Violence in America: A Public Health Approach*. New York: Oxford University Press, 1991.

Schorr, L. *Common Purpose: Strengthening Families and Neighborhoods to Build America*. New York: Anchor Books, Doubleday, 1997.

Simon, D., and E. Burns. *The Corner: A Year in the Life of an Inner-City Neighborhood*. New York: Broadway Books, 1997.

Skogan, W. *Disorder and Decline: Crime and Spiral of Decay in American Neighborhoods*. New York: Free Press, 1990.

Towers, G. *Building Democracy: Community Architecture in the Inner Cities*. London: UCL Press Limited, 1995.

Walter, E. *Placeways: A Theory of the Human Environment*. Chapel Hill: The University of North Carolina Press, 1988.

Wilson, J. *Bureaucracy: What Government Agencies Do and Why They Do It*. New York: Basic Books, 1989.

Index

About the Author

Michael Greenberg, professor and codirector of the New Jersey Graduate Program in Public Health of Rutgers University and the University of Medicine and Dentistry of New Jersey, studies environmental health policies. His books include *Urbanization and Cancer Mortality* (1983), *Hazardous Waste Sites: The Credibility Gap* (1984), *Public Health and the Environment* (1987), and *Environmental Risk and the Press* (1987). His most recent book is *Environmentally Devastated Neighborhoods in the United States* (1996). He has contributed more than three hundred publications to scientific journals such as *Cancer Research* and the *American Journal of Epidemiology* and to public interest periodicals like *Society*, *The Sciences*, and *Public Interest*. He is currently a member of the National Research Council committee that oversees the destruction of the U.S. chemical-weapons stockpile. Greenberg is director of the National Center for Neighborhood and Brownfields Redevelopment at Rutgers University.